D0069079

The Step-parent's Survival Guide

Positive advice for achieving
a successful step-family

Hilary Boyd

WARD LOCK

A Ward Lock Book

First published in the UK 1998 by
Ward Lock
Wellington House
125 Strand
London
WC2R 0BB

A Cassell Imprint

Reprinted 1999

Distributed in the United States by
Sterling Publishing Co. Inc.
387 Park Avenue South
New York
NY 10016-8810, USA

British Library Cataloguing-in-Publication Data
A catalogue record for this book is available from
the British Library

ISBN 0-7063-7732-X

Designed and typeset by Tim Higgins
Edited by Annie Lee

Printed and bound in Great Britain
by Mackays of Chatham

The Step-parent's Survival Guide

Contents

Preface

I began my parenting existence as a part-time step-parent twenty-five years ago, then became a parent to my two daughters, then moved on to full-time step-parenting seven years later, so I've seen it all! My stepdaughter and I have been through so much together as we adjusted to our new family structure, everything from anxiety about whether, and how, it would work, to fear that it wasn't working, to resentment that we had to make the effort, and finally to acceptance and integration. We have cried and shouted and laughed in the attempt, and made many mistakes ... But ... every tear was worth it. We are now a family and I dedicate this book to that family, but particularly to my stepdaughter, Amanda. I wouldn't be without her.

CHAPTER 1

What is a stepfamily?

What do we mean by 'a family'?

Before the Second World War the members of a family living together, or in close proximity, commonly made up a diverse group, often including grandparents, parents, in-laws and un-married siblings, or families that had been reconstructed because of spousal death. The 1950s, with the Welfare State, medical advances such as the discovery of penicillin and an overall improvement in the standard of living, saw a decline in the death rate. Economic migration also accelerated with the means of travel both easier and cheaper, encouraging people to leave their birth-place in greater numbers than before and set up smaller family units, often many miles from their relatives.

This smaller unit or 'nuclear family' was seized upon by the burgeoning television advertising industry of the fifties as a very convenient marketing device. 'Family' was now invested with a definite article, 'the', and 'The Family' was packaged and presented to the public as a sweet, wholesome, happy group consisting of a mother, a father and two, possibly three children. Suddenly there was the family car, the family house and the family holiday, every-thing packaged with the family in mind and therefore emphasizing the neat, 'nuclear family' consisting of two *happy* parents and two *happy* children. These post-war children learnt to read with books that backed up this image, watched television which assumed it and, unlike subsequent generations, were quite unfamiliar with divorce. Public figures, even Hollywood stars, strove to present the required 'happy family' as a backdrop to their public life.

But we cannot entirely blame the media. The aspirations and values of any society are mirrored, as well as influenced, by its media, but this sort of stereotyping fixed an ideal in people's minds which was based on the false premise that the only 'good' family is the 'conventional' family. (For the purposes of this book I will use 'conventional' to describe a family consisting of two parents and their biological children, whether married or not.) It was only in the late fifties and early sixties that social realism began to creep into the literature and theatre of the time, with so-called 'kitchen sink' dramas such as John Osborne's *Look Back in Anger* and novels such as John Braine's *Room at the Top* and Alan Sillitoe's *Saturday Night and Sunday Morning*.

As divorce became easier and easier to obtain over the next decade, divorce rates saw a gradual, perhaps inevitable, increase until today, thirty years later, at least one in three marriages will end in divorce. With remarriage rates also soaring, the number of adults and children involved in both part-time and full-time stepfamilies has now reached the millions, yet despite these facts the yearning for the 'good', and therefore 'conventional', family persists. Perhaps we should ask ourselves today whether this post-war media-endorsed image ever really existed, or whether it was merely a necessary refuge created by a generation shaken and destabilized by a horrific war, anxious to create at least the image of social harmony, thus imbuing the term 'family' with a dangerous burden of value.

Even today we have been so conditioned to believe in this ideal that, despite the reality of divorce and remarriage rates, families that do not conform can be unfairly stigmatized and cited, without adequate research, as the root cause of juvenile violence, truancy, child abuse and low educational achievement. Whereas the trauma, distress and disruption a child suffers on parental divorce, separation or death cannot be underestimated, it is neither true nor helpful to suggest that all children suffer irreparable damage from the experience. The family unit, however constructed, is a very complex entity and can be a source of great nurturing and support or extreme violence and neglect and all permutations between, but this is true both of the 'conventional' family and of the family which has been divided and/or reconstructed for whatever reason.

What do we mean by a stepfamily?

The National Stepfamily Association, launched in 1983 in Britain, offers this definition:

> A stepfamily is created when two adults, one or both of whom already has a child(ren), form a new relationship where the new partner becomes an important adult and parental figure to the child(ren).
>
> Stepfamilies may be preceded by bereavement, single parenthood, separation or divorce and may arise through cohabitation, marriage or remarriage.
>
> Stepchildren may be full-time or part-time members of the household.

New legislation

Aside from the emotional adjustments that confront a stepfamily, there are also legal and financial considerations. New legislation over the last ten years has begun to acknowledge the changing nature of today's family, with divorce and remarriage (and in many cases the breakdown of the remarriage) being taken into account. In such a complex arena it is hardly surprising that this legislation is, in turn, helpful and obstructive to the stepfamilies it is designed to support. However, the emphasis is more and more about parents using counselling and mediation services when deciding on parenting arrangements for their children post divorce, rather than leaving it to the litigious machinations of the lawyers. This not only benefits the children involved, but can also reduce the hostility between the separating parents by allowing them to air their differences safely in the presence of a neutral third party.

Stepfamilies are all about balance. Somehow the needs (emotional, legal and financial) of the new family must be balanced against the similar ongoing needs of the original family. All too frequently unresolved conflicts and jealousies make the chance of achieving this balance impossible, at least in the short term, to the detriment of all concerned. Organizations are now springing up which offer telephone helplines and comprehensive information on all aspects of step-parenting to address these issues and offer help and support as never before for today's stepfamily.

The role of the step-parent

Stepfamilies are different from 'conventional' families, that is a fact. What is not a fact is that stepfamilies are necessarily always worse than 'conventional' families. A step-parent is basically an adult who forms a relationship with a parent, and this is where much of the problem lies. He does not enter the family because of the child, but because of the adult, and often the child's presence is sidelined or even ignored when a stepfamily is formed, the focus remaining very much on the importance of the adult romance and interrelation. Another of the problems with step-parenting is that, to date, the role of the step-parent has been ill-defined. Most people recognize the basic responsibilities of parents towards their children, but how much responsibility does, or should, a step-parent have? Should he discipline the child, financially support the child, make lifestyle decisions for the child as a parent might do, or should he leave this entirely, or in part, to the parents? If he does take on some or all of these parental responsibilities, then who is the child to look to as the ultimate authority – a resident step-parent or an absent parent?

This ambivalence is one of the root causes of conflict in step-families, as it muddies the waters for both the adults and children concerned. Most children join stepfamilies between the ages of four and ten these days, which means that a step-parent can be taking on a very young family, with many years of full-time parenting to go. This suggests that clarification of roles and expectations at an early stage in a new relationship, followed by constant re-evaluation, would be a sensible route to take, but adults are strangely reluctant to set boundaries or define even the parenting role, let alone that of step-parenting. Child-rearing has been perceived by society as a natural process which demands no education, a task to which we instinctively adapt and ought to be instinctively suited. Although this perception is slowly changing, there is still a peculiar denial of the problems of parenting, which lays an enormous burden of guilt upon those of us who feel we are failing or those who are frightened of failing, and often prevents us seeking help until perhaps the child starts to manifest some signs of disturbance such as truanting or antisocial behaviour in the classroom.

This denial is surprising, given the huge emphasis today on the consequences of 'bad' parenting. During the last few years the media has been bulging with stories of child abuse, False Memory Syndrome, children murdering children, nannies who abuse babies because the task of surrogate parenting is too onerous, teenage violence and violence in schools, most of which is laid at the door of 'bad' parents, a conveniently demonized section of the population to which we, of course, do not belong. Yet do any of us really know what being a 'good' parent means, or if indeed there is such a person, any more than there is a 'good' family? Maybe in the past, when children grew up in extended families in communities where everyone enjoyed an extensive support network, it was easier to be a parent, but perhaps we need to re-evaluate modern parenting in the light of the nuclear family, working mothers, divorce and remarriage and accept that it is no longer such a natural, instinctive process, that today's parents need education and support and freedom from the stigma attached to not being able to cope. If we could open the debate and begin to focus on what makes a 'good enough' parent, to use Bruno Bettelheim's phrase, rather than sensationalizing the 'bad', we might reduce the negative consequences for children in the future.

The nurturing structures which make for 'good enough' parenting are essentially the same as the nurturing structures which make for 'good enough' step-parenting, with the obvious difference that a step-parent steps into a ready-made family, and a process which normally takes place over many years, from conception through birth and early childhood, allowing time to develop these parenting structures, is missing. A stepfamily can be created overnight, but the perils of rushing into the creation of a stepfamily and the problems that can arise from not considering the role and level of commitment of the incoming step-parent carefully enough, or acknowledging the difference between the role of natural parent and that of a step-parent, cannot be underestimated.

When does a person become a step-parent?

This is a very difficult area and one which can cause much unhappiness, particularly for the children concerned, if handled insensitively. Legally, a person only becomes a step-parent when he marries a parent, but since marriage is not necessarily a desired option, a step-parent also becomes an unofficial step-parent when he makes a full-time commitment to a parent with a child, whether residential or not. In the non-residential situation trouble can arise if a parent and his new partner employ the title 'step-parent' before the child concerned is ready to accept it. It is perhaps for the child to decide when he feels ready to call his parent's new partner his step-parent, and this can take time while the adult and child gradually begin to recognize and accept that they have to take each other seriously as relations. In the residential situation a partner might be said to become a step-parent when he takes up residence with the family, but again it is wise not to impose specific labels such as 'step-parent' and 'step-child' too soon, but rather to allow the child to come to this realization in time. Unfortunately some children have to deal with a succession of transient 'step-parents', who although resident with their parent for a period hardly merit the name.

Children are at risk from stepfathers as well as the traditionally 'wicked' stepmother

The often quoted legend of the wicked stepmother, which has been enshrined in literature since the advent of the fairy-tale, has been largely replaced in modern times by that of the wicked stepfather. Men have always remarried more frequently than women, for various reasons, but historically remarriage followed the death, often in childbirth, of the woman. Today, with the main reason for remarriage being divorce and with the majority of women still alive and retaining primary care of their children following separation, the majority of full-time stepfamilies are in fact stepfather households.

Two recent research studies, one by Martin Daly and Margot Wilson from McMasters University in Ontario, Canada, in 1996, and the other by the National Society for the Prevention of Cruelty to Children in Britain in 1992, make alarming reading on the subject of the high levels of child abuse, both physical and sexual, perpetrated on children by their stepfathers. A debate has ensued about the nature of these and other current research studies, with some experts pointing out that they have mostly been carried out on families already identified as high risk, perhaps from alcohol or drug abuse. This is mainly because research using the stepfamily unit is difficult to undertake because of the fluid nature of child residency and the dissolving and recreating of families post divorce and separation. Nonetheless, the results of these studies are very important and cannot be ignored, though it must also be said that child protection is not going to be well served by dumping all the blame on to one easily identified group of adults at the expense of the wider picture. Are wicked stepmothers now a thing of the past? Are the abusing stepfathers long-term or transitory in the child's life? Can we ever know the extent of sexual abuse and violence in 'conventional' families? More research, open debate and support facilities are needed to inform those involved in child-rearing about how to avoid situations which might prove in any way dangerous to the child.

The child in the stepfamily

There are certain truths about a small child which define his perception of his parents and the family structure. When a family separates and a child is faced with a reconstructed family, a parent and step-parent's understanding of these truths can help the child to accept his new situation more easily. Parents tend to shy away from a child's pain because it is too hard to contemplate, especially in the context of their own trauma, but given the right help a child can, in time, adapt and be happy in a stepfamily. Step-parents can ease the path for a new stepchild by being aware of some of the following truths:

> * **A child does not see his parents as divisible.** He needs reassurance that, although his mother and father are living separately and step-parents are on the cards, his parents will always, no matter what, be his parents.

> * **A small child has no yardstick by which to measure his parents.** If his parents argue and fight all the time

then that is what parents do and it is not, in his eyes, a reasonable excuse for destroying his security. Parents must be prepared for him not to understand.

* **A child's world is very small.** He regards himself as the originator of everything (remember the game when he covers his eyes and can't see, so thinks you can't see him?), so he must also be the cause. Parents often fail to realize how much responsibility a child takes for the breakdown of his parents' marriage.

* **A child wants conformity.** He wants a mother and father at home. It takes time, more than most adults realize, for a child to accept that this is no longer the case or that a stepfamily is an acceptable substitute.

* **A child has no autonomy.** His parents don't come to him and say: 'Do you mind if we get divorced? We won't if you do.' Or 'Do you mind if I'm in love with this stranger?' This can make a child feel impotent and angry. Within the context of separation and a subsequent stepfamily a child can be consulted and given practical choices.

* **A child almost always harbours the hope that his parents will eventually be reconciled.** Divorced parents cannot change this, but they can recognize it.

* **A child craves parental approval.** He will often say what he thinks a parent wants to hear, e.g. 'I hate my stepmother,' or 'I think you should marry so-and-so.' He is testing his parents and what he says must be listened to, but not always taken at face value.

* **A child can sniff out a lie at twenty paces.** A parent or step-parent should always treat their child with honesty and respect.

* **A child sees and hears much more than most adults realize.** A parent must never underestimate how much a child is taking in what is happening around him. Many children are more traumatized by what happens before the separation than by the separation itself. Often the child hears his parent talking on the phone to her partner or friends about things he should not hear, is a silent presence during arguments, and sees things he should not see.

* **A child does not require material compensation for emotional trauma.** Showering a child with presents because of guilt only stores up trouble for everyone in the future. Nothing is a substitute for real parenting commitment.

This book aims to pinpoint the areas where so many stepfamilies go wrong and to offer some practical suggestions and modifications to help achieve the balance I referred to earlier. It won't be easy to achieve, but neither is it impossible, and please remember: *You are not alone!*

CHAPTER 2

Step-parent meets stepchild

The first encounter between step-parent and stepchild can affect the whole nature of the stepfamily relationship which follows. Everyone who comes to the meeting can arrive laden with all sorts of emotional baggage, including hopes, expectations, pre-conceived notions, prejudices, jealousies and insecurities. This first encounter, if well managed, can get everyone off to a good start, but equally, if badly managed, it can serve to drive home those potential prejudices, jealousies and insecurities, setting up a whole range of problems in the future, most of which are avoidable with careful planning and an awareness of the potential pitfalls.

Let's look at it first *from the child's point of view.*

Too soon

This may seem an obvious thing to say, but it is surprising how often parents make this fundamental mistake. A child who has just experienced the trauma of his parents' divorce is in a very vulnerable state. The last thing he needs is to be confronted by another emotional entanglement, especially one which may affect his whole childhood so fundamentally. To introduce a future step-parent within weeks or even months of a separation is to jeopardize that step-relationship for ever, and this fact cannot be over-emphasized. For a start the child has not even begun to come to terms with his parents being apart, and, secondly, he will immediately associate the new adult with his parents' split (sometimes with reason) and thus with his own distress. Lastly he may identify the lover as a barrier to the parental reconciliation he longs for.

There is no magic time-scale, but it is generally agreed that children take two to five years to recover from losing a parent, either by separation or by death. Patience and consideration of the child's progress at this stage can save serious problems in the future. The average child does want to see a parent happy, and after a reasonable time can welcome the advent of a parent's new partner.

It was nearly four years since Wendy's father had left and Wendy remembers she and her brother felt like a 'shipwrecked family', rootless and adrift, worried about the responsibility they felt for their lonely mother. The children, both in their early teens by then, had frequent whispered conversations late into the night about the possibility of their mother ever meeting someone else. If ever she went out they would cross-question her for hours about who she met and whether or not she liked them until it became something of a joke. When Patrick finally appeared Wendy prayed every night that he would stay.

Wendy remembers vividly getting in a panic one night before her mother went out.

> She had put on a truly hideous, frumpy, mustard-yellow dress with polka dots for her second date with this gorgeous man, Patrick, and she swirled in front of me and asked what I thought. I knew she had just bought the dress and I didn't have the heart to say it was gross, but I was utterly convinced that Patrick would take one look at her and never be seen again. I was so desperate for her to be happy. He stayed though, thank God, and it transpired much later that he adored the dress, which perhaps says more for his commitment than his taste. I don't think we'd have been so keen if he'd shown up earlier though, it would have caused trouble for everyone.

Where and how

Children very quickly pick up on tension in the adults around them and, whether teenaged or younger, can react badly to it, especially if they feel they are somehow being scrutinized and put to the test. A parent, longing for her lover and her child to bond because she knows how much hangs on them doing so, too often opts for an intimate, special setting in the hope that this will signal the importance of the event and give them both proper time to 'get to know each other', the result being unnatural formality, tension and pressure, with exactly the opposite effect to the one she is trying to achieve.

Jed remembers with some shame the first night he was introduced to his future stepmother. His father came to pick him up at his mother's house and immediately berated Jed, fifteen at the time, for his jeans and trainers. When Jed explained that he didn't have any other kind of clothes and anyway what did it matter, his father flew into a nervous funk and dragged him to his cupboard, throwing his son's chaotic piles of crumpled clothes all over the room. When it was finally established that Jed had spoken the truth, his father went downstairs and began to yell at his ex-wife for the state of his son's wardrobe. She then shouted back that if he gave them more money she might do something about it, and the row developed into a full-blown marital war until everyone was in a foul mood and Jed was still in his jeans and trainers.

When they arrived at an extremely grand restaurant in town to meet his father's girlfriend, they were turned away because of Jed's jeans and trainers and had to go and eat in an altogether less attractive establishment down the road. Jed admits that by this time he was in a heavy, monosyllabic teenage sulk brought on by a mixture of guilt and resentment, and could hardly bear even to look at the woman his father was in love with. They had wine with the meal, and, not surprisingly, Jed got drunk. He vaguely remembers his father's girlfriend asking him polite questions about school, him grunting in reply and his father looking as if he might disinteg-rate with rage, but Jed's pièce de resistance was still to come: on the journey home he vomited all over the back seat of his father's car.

He didn't have much to do with his stepmother for some time after that, but as adults they have managed to build a friendly relationship and now they all laugh about 'the night from hell'.

To avoid such intensity it makes sense to opt for a more informal occasion for the first meeting, preferably with other people present, such as a small family party or a weekend lunch with friends, where everyone feels relaxed and under no pressure to perform or live up to any expectations. Subsequent encounters can also be of this nature, until the child and adult concerned have built up a natural friendship which can act as a good basis for any future relationship. There is no hurry.

Lack of emotional support

When adults fall in love and plan to commit to a relationship for the first time there are not usually any children involved. They can spend their days in a state of glorious obsession, holding hands and kissing at will, staring into each other's eyes, devoting every minute to each other in thought, word and deed. When a separated parent falls in love there usually *are* children involved. This can mean that a child who may have been the parent's only focus up till that minute suddenly finds herself in the presence of an unwanted adult who appears to claim most of her parent's attention. Whatever age the child is, and however long the time since the separation, if during these first meetings with a future step-parent her parent withdraws too much of his normal atten-tion the child will resent it, and the focus of the resentment will be the step-parent.

Obviously the child will have to learn to share his parent again, but this can be a gradual process, and it is hoped that the added attention from the step-parent will be some compensation.

Jamie's father had been alone for about a year when he met Victoria. Jamie, aged twelve, says that in that year his father had been 'perfect', always turning up to take him for the weekend and devoting the entire time to Jamie's obsession, football. He says they had the 'sort of fun men have together' that doesn't involve too much clearing up or eating the right thing or going to bed on time, but his father was 'always responsible, not wild or anything' about his homework and always got him home punctually on Sunday nights.

Then Vicky appeared. Jamie says:

> I wouldn't have minded in theory having a stepmother because I didn't like to think of Dad on his own, but suddenly he started being late to pick me up and we stopped going to football so much because 'Vicky didn't like it', and if we did then Dad didn't want us to discuss the match afterwards the way we did before because 'Vicky doesn't understand all this football stuff'. I wasn't allowed to stay up in the evenings and sometimes Dad even cancelled the weekend altogether, saying he was working, which I didn't believe. Vicky was perfectly nice I suppose, but she just took Dad over and it got so as I hated her. I behaved like a little bastard I know, really rebellious and rude, but I felt so let down and bereft without my dad. If he had just taken a bit more time for me to adjust I know it would have helped. I sort of lost touch for a while, I didn't want to see him with her. It's better now I guess, but never the same. You can't do one thing with a kid one day, then change everything without any warning the next and expect the kid to take it, it's not fair.

Overt sexual behaviour

Because being in love often means displays of overt sexuality that a child may not have been used to from his parents, very often the first real inkling a child has that the new adult with his parent is anything other than a friend is when he witnesses one of these displays. Unfortunately this may mean finding a strange man in bed with his mother when he wakes in the night or early in the morning, it may be a passionate kiss or merely holding hands or sitting entwined on the sofa. It may be difficult for a parent to regulate her life so as to avoid this happening, but it is better to wait until the relationship is more established from the child's point of view before he sees such demonstrations of affection. And by the way, parents, in case you didn't know, do *not* have sex.

Parents also make the mistake of thinking that because their child might know and like the adult they are in love with in another context, that child will automatically cope with a swift transition to displays of physical affection. This is not true. A child might adore his father's best friend, but not when he's suddenly in bed with the child's mother.

Ruth and Andrew had Ruth's divorced sister and her ten-year-old daughter to stay at their cottage in the country. The sister had asked if her boyfriend could also be invited, under the pretence that the man was a business associate of Andrew's. Although Ruth was reluctant, she acquiesced for her niece's sake. The first day the niece got on well with her mother's boyfriend, he made her laugh and paid her a good deal of attention.

The next morning, however, a very sheepish pair greeted Ruth and apologized profusely for exposing her to their love-making the previous night, which had apparently been very inventive and had taken place on the sofa in the sitting-room. Ruth was baffled – she had seen and heard nothing, the cottage walls were thick.

'But we saw you standing by the door,' Ruth's sister exclaimed.
'Not me,' Ruth insisted.

*They all realized to their horror that Ruth's niece, who bore
a passing resemblance to her aunt, must have been witness to her
mother's antics with her boyfriend. Every subsequent effort
the boyfriend made to return to the easy relationship he and the
girl had enjoyed the previous day failed, and eventually the
two adults parted company.*

Lack of choice

As adults we have the opportunity to make our own choices.
We can choose where we go, who we meet, who we like and
choose to spend time with, and what we wear. This is not so much
the case with children – they often have to fit into an adult structure to make life manageable, but they can still be consulted and
offered choices within that structure. For children who have lost
the security of their original family this is particularly important,
as being included in the decision-making process gives them back
the feeling of being in control of their life. Tanya was not so lucky:

*A few weeks after Tanya's father had left home he arrived at the
house one Saturday morning, unannounced. (She thinks now that
her mother was too distressed at the time to know how to tell
her and was resistant to the access visits anyway.) Tanya remembers
being thrilled to see him and thinking he had come home for
good. She thought he would take her to the park and then to the
supermarket, their usual Saturday ritual together which she very
much enjoyed, but he announced that they were going to the zoo
and that she should wear the pink dress he had bought her the
day before he had left. She hated it, it reminded her of him leaving,
but she dutifully complied.*

*On the way to the zoo her father told her about his friend, who
he said was beautiful and charming and loved children and was
very special, urging Tanya to like her, be nice to her and behave. She
will never forget the first sighting of her future stepmother:*

Dad had said she was beautiful and very special and I had been expecting nothing less than Marilyn Monroe, but Jenny was just really ordinary. She had jeans on and a T-shirt, hair in a pony-tail . . . I was so disappointed . . . and angry she was there at all.

'This is Jenny,' my father said. 'She's very sad at the moment and so I thought we'd take her to the zoo to cheer her up.' Jenny didn't look even remotely sad, in fact she spent the whole day laughing and smiling at Dad in such an intimate way that I'd have to have been brain dead not to have smelt a rat, even at six. They took me to see Guy the Gorilla, and while I was looking at him through the glass I saw Dad's and Jenny's reflection . . . kissing passionately. I did nothing, said nothing, didn't even turn round, but I remember freezing with horror. The day was ruined of course, and I hated Jenny . . . really hated her. On the way home Dad looked really pleased with himself.

'So, did you like her, sweetheart? She's wonderful, isn't she?' I said nothing – what was there to say? But he persisted: 'You did like her, didn't you? She's very special to me and it's important you like her . . . we'll be seeing a lot of her and it would be better if you liked her. Oh, and sweetheart, it's probably best you don't tell Mummy that Jenny came with us today.'

I was so bewildered. Instinct told me that Mum wouldn't like me meeting Jenny, but I wasn't clear why or what exactly was going on, only that this beastly woman had ruined my life and that Dad would be angry if I didn't like her. How could I like her, she'd stolen my Dad?

It would be foolish to suggest that parents give their children endless choices; nothing would ever get done. Whereas realistically Tanya could have no choice in her parents' decision to split up, she was not too young to be included in at least part of the day's plans. Her mother could have warned Tanya that her father was coming round, and that he was paying a visit, not returning to the family. Her father could have asked her where she wanted to go and what she wanted to do, he could have let her wear whatever she felt most comfortable in, he could have asked her if she minded someone else coming with them, and, if he had decided to introduce his new girlfriend, he could have allowed her to make up her own mind about whether she liked her or not. This isn't spoiling, it's respect.

Now let's look at that first encounter *from the adult's point of view.* Because parents are responsible for their child's well-being it is easy to condemn them when things go wrong, without making an attempt to understand how difficult it is for them to reconcile their own happiness with the happiness of their children when trying to remake their lives after separation and divorce.

Being in love

It is human nature for a person to want a close, loving relationship. Unfortunately the process of falling in love is a notoriously obsessive process, which is hardly diminished by the presence of children. Samuel Johnson once famously observed that remarriage, after the demise of an unsuccessful one, was 'the triumph of hope over experience', but people continue to hope and to crave the stability and comforts of family life. The combination of this hope and the obsessive quality of being in love can catapult a normally thoughtful parent into rash behaviour with regard to existing children.

This is never more true than at the point of introduction between a child and her future step-parent. It is understandable when a person falls madly in love that they want immediately to share someone as important as their own child with the object of their affection, and it is also understandable that they might assume, because they love them both, that they will therefore love each other. Most people will recognize the situation when a friend says: 'I'm dying to introduce you to so-and-so, she's my oldest friend and I know you'll adore her.' You meet the woman and loathe her on sight, quite unable to imagine how your friend can be close to such a frightful person. As with friends, so possibly with children and step-parents. The fact that the parent loves both her child and her new partner unfortunately doesn't mean they will even like each other, but it is true that, if the circumstances of introduction are right, the tensions a hasty or forced encounter imposes will not add unnecessary antipathy.

Martin remembers a similar situation to poor Tanya's first encounter. He had no children of his own, and was still unsure whether he wanted any, when he met Sarah and fell in love. She had two children by her first marriage, a boy and a girl then aged seven and five. From the start she was keen for him to meet them, extolling their virtues, showing him snapshots, and although he loved her he insisted he was not yet ready to involve himself in their lives.

Sarah ignored his protestations; she was literally unable to imagine that he wouldn't love the children on sight, and one day, when she had arranged to meet Martin at the pub they frequented, she took her children along with her. Martin was furious:

> I couldn't believe she had done it, not just to me but to her children too. Of course I tried to make the best of it, but the kids were appalling . . . rude, undisciplined, constantly nagging and interrupting Sarah, but worst of all . . . I found them utterly charmless. I felt so ashamed of thinking this about two innocent kids, but I just couldn't help it.
>
> Sarah could see I wasn't enjoying them and started making excuses, saying they weren't usually as bad as this and that they'd both just had colds, and to a certain extent I believed her, and the combination of not being prepared and being angry with her for springing it on me didn't

exactly help, but neither the children nor I recovered from the experience. I just knew I couldn't be a good step-father to them and they clearly weren't ready for one either. Me and Sarah went out for a while longer, but the kids thing got in the way in the end.

On reflection, Martin isn't sure whether he would have felt differently if he had been given more time and preparation to get used to the idea of Sarah's children, but he is definite that that first meeting had a very detrimental effect for the following reasons:

* Because Martin was angry with Sarah, and, by association, with her children. (He's not proud of this, but says it's a fact.)

* Because Sarah had not been long out of her relationship with the children's father Martin feels he was not seeing them at their best and that their rudeness and aggression was perhaps transitory and understandable, though nonetheless alienating at the time.

* The guilt Martin felt (and thousands of step-parents experience this) at not immediately liking Sarah's children was a further barrier to their relationship. Disliking a child is a particularly uncomfortable experience for an adult, as children are somehow perceived as whole-some, uncomplicated and innocent. As we all know, this is not always the case.

* Martin saw the pub that they met in as their own place, the place where he and Sarah gazed into each other's eyes and held hands, not a venue for badly behaved children. He realizes this is selfish; after all, he knew Sarah had children when he met her (a fact that didn't bother him in theory) and he says he is surprised, looking back, that so much could have turned on that one event, but he is ashamed to admit that it did.

Sarah could have helped their cause considerably by waiting for a time when her children were more relaxed and receptive to the idea of a stepfather. She could also have taken Martin's doubts seriously, and so avoided forcing him into a corner and making him reluctant.

'Hello, I'm your new step-parent!'

One of the problems when a new partner is introduced to children on a one-to-one basis is how they should greet each other. Again the expectations of the parent often intrude, putting both stepchild and step-parent in a position of false intimacy.

Jane remembers her partner, Callum, keeping her away from his children for years in case he hurt them or his ex-partner, but finally the day came. Callum didn't want the two children, then aged four and seven, to meet Jane for the first time in the car, so he dropped her off at a local hotel, then went to pick them up on his own. Although Jane understood the logic of this, it made her feel some-how alien and unacceptable. The children arrived at the hotel, and Callum immediately said to the children: 'This is Jane, go and give her a big kiss.' The children complied, of course, but Jane could see that his daughter, the elder of the two, was surprised and reluctant to be asked to kiss a total stranger, particularly one she had not known existed until five minutes before, and Jane felt very awkward because she also was not accustomed to kissing a child she had just met. The whole thing got off to a bad start, with both children immediately wary of Jane. She wishes now that, after the huge length of time they had waited to make this introduction, they had had more discussion as to how they would actually conduct it.

Callum could have made it much more casual. Ideally it would have been easier for them all if they had met in a gathering with other people, but if this was the only way possible because of distance and time it would have been better for him to say something simple, such as: 'This is Jane, she's a friend of mine.' This puts no pressure on anyone.

Another example is Alisa's experience:

Alisa remembers meeting her stepmother, Barbara, for the first time when she was sixteen. She was living in America at the time, and her father and Barbara arranged a meeting at their hotel room. Alisa and her younger sister went along without any particular prejudice against Barbara, but when they arrived Barbara threw her arms around them and presented them both with expensive gifts. Alisa's was a leather shoulder bag. Both the girls were offended at what they saw as 'sucking up' from someone they considered a total stranger.

It may seem that a step-parent can't win, but the truth is that they cannot lose if they resist any influence their partner might bring to bear to behave in any way out of the ordinary with their stepchildren. If they treat them as they would a friend's child, with politeness and respect, then at least they are giving both themselves and the child the best chance for the relationship to develop in its own time.

The 'pink dress' syndrome

Perhaps because parents can't help seeing their children as extensions of themselves, as display models who reflect their status and beliefs, they frequently cause rows and torment their children about their form of dress, and never more so than when introducing their children to important strangers. This is not the exclusive preserve of the separated family, far from it, but time after time research has shown that, like Jed's jeans and trainers and Tanya's pink dress, when parents are introducing their children to their lovers they make ridiculous attempts to at best polish them up, at worst re-create them.

In some cases this may be because, having fallen out with the parent with whom the child now resides, they are trying to erase that parent's influence, but more commonly it is a futile attempt to create the 'perfect child', the child who is most likely, they think, in their delusion, to be acceptable to their lover.

This ploy on the part of the parent is doomed to failure. A parent must let his child stand or fall, as we all must, by who he is. Dressing him in clothes which make him uncomfortable and do not reflect his personality will only make him angry and resentful, especially when he perceives that the reason for his parent's sudden dissatisfaction with his appearance is linked to an introduction to his future step-parent. It will only be another nail in that poor step-parent's coffin.

Melanie, fourteen at the time, shudders as she remembers the white tights her father bought her to go with a skirt and blouse he wanted her to wear when she met the woman he was in love with. She admits to being a little jealous but not entirely averse to the idea of her father being in a relationship – her mother had been remarried for years – but seeing the white tights made her take an instant dislike to someone she had so far never met. If her father thought this woman would want her dressed like this then she was convinced they could never get on.

Melanie's habitual clothes were, like all her friends, jeans, heavy shirts and desert boots, but she insists she always looked clean and tidy, and her father had never had a problem before. Now she had a dilemma: should she disobey him and wear her normal clothes, or struggle into the prissy white tights and pretend she was someone else? After much debate she decided to stick to her jeans and risk his wrath. He was very angry, and what hurt her most was that she realized the woman actually didn't care how she looked, it was her father who had found her wanting and for some reason desired a different kind of daughter, perhaps to go with his different kind of life. It took her a long time to reconcile her feelings from that night.

Many parents feel justified in dictating to their children what sort of person they should be. A parent may influence his children, but he cannot determine the result of that influence. Children are individuals in the same way as adults are and should be loved and respected accordingly. Step-parents can help both their new partner and his child in this situation by insisting on a relaxed and informal attitude to the first meeting.

Understanding a parent's need to protect their child

It is always hard for any parent to fathom how much a child is capable of understanding what is going on in his mind, particularly when the parent is also under emotional strain or turmoil. Separated parents, with no other adult at home to interact with, will often burden their offspring with too much emotional baggage, especially an eldest or only child. Others shut themselves off from their children, certain they are too young to understand any part of the turmoil, and risk leaving them bewildered and insecure about what is happening to the family. It is difficult to get the right balance.

There are a few specific questions which a future step-parent should think about with his new partner to help him deal with his future stepchild successfully, such as:

* How much does the child know about why the parental marriage broke down?

* How much does and should the child know about his parent's feelings for a new partner?

* How can a parent and her new partner know when the child concerned is ready to meet the new partner?

* How much should a parent and her new partner warn a child about plans for the future?

Different circumstances require different responses, depending on, for instance, the age of the child and the length of time since the separation, but the general rule of thumb is not to dump too much unsolicited information of an emotional nature on to a child, whether it concerns the past, the present or the future. If and when the child asks questions, a parent should answer them as honestly as she can, giving the child sufficient time to understand the reply fully, and should guard against him picking up snippets of conversations she might be having on the phone or with friends which can be taken out of context and misinterpreted. There are no rigid rules for when an introduction can take place, but if a parent watches and assesses her child's state of mind she will know when the time is right; if she is going too fast there is no need to worry, the child will soon let her know! No parent should ever use a child as a go-between to inflict pain on the separated partner by feeding information about her new circumstances that she knows will be passed on, or by asking the child to keep secrets about her lifestyle from his other parent.

What children really want to know is how their life will be affected; they are less interested in the ups and downs of a parent's emotional state, except in the way it directly affects themselves, but they appreciate practical information such as who will live with whom, where they will live, whether their schooling or friendships will have to change and how often they will see the absent parent.

Janice's experience with her father's girlfriend had been good initially. They had met often at her aunt's house and Janice liked her, and had begun to accept that she was close to her father, but one day she heard her aunt and her future stepmother discussing wedding plans, even the role Janice would play as a bridesmaid. Janice had no notion until that moment that marriage was on the cards and was extremely upset, particularly when she confronted her father later and he completely denied it. She accepts now that all the adults involved probably thought they had her best interests at heart by not being more open with her, but she feels that she was old enough at ten to be able to understand the truth and accept it. The deceit soured her relationship with both her stepmother and her father for a considerable time to come, and she remembers the wedding itself with great unhappiness.

Too many step-parents

This one is simple. No child needs to be faced with introductions to all the adults his parent might take a passing fancy to. A parent should spare the child until she is sure this person is really important to her. Obviously things go wrong and this cannot be helped, but both a parent and her lover ought to be as sure as possible of their commitment before allowing a close relationship to develop with a child. The child from a separated family has had to deal with enough loss already.

To summarize:

* Make sure you and your future stepchild are not rushed into the first introduction. A lot depends on it.

* When the time is right, use relaxed gatherings of friends and family to make the introduction.

* Help your partner understand that you have no expectations with regard to his child. Trainers are fine!

* Don't allow the prefix 'step' to be used until you are sure the child is comfortable with the new relationship.

* Involve the child as much as possible in plans which affect him.

* Help your partner to maintain his normal routine with his child in the early stages, without intruding.

* Be honest, but don't burden a child unnecessarily with information about a new relationship.

* Don't involve a child in a relationship until you are both serious.

So when at last the members of the stepfamily-in-the-making have all met, what happens next? Read on.

CHAPTER 3

Potential conflict in the new stepfamily

All families have conflict, everything including sibling rivalry, children resenting parental authority, arguments about money, parents angry at a child's independence, or parents fighting between themselves. It would be a very abnormal family that did not have this strife, to a greater or lesser extent, at some time during the children's childhood. Britain, unfortunately, unlike some other cultures, has a lamentable history of repression about emotional conflict, the attitude 'Don't talk about it and it will go away' still prevailing, despite the atmosphere of personal revelation and exposure which has begun to filter across the Atlantic from North America in recent years. Excessive disgorging of emotion to anyone passing cannot be recommended, but families in general would certainly benefit from acknowledging the conflicts in family life as natural and so giving themselves permission to air their differences before these differences become resentment and then anger.

Stepfamilies have specific areas of potential conflict and rivalry which stem from their complex structure, and it is important to recognize what these areas are in order to be able to deal with them before they get out of hand:

> * The jealousy and rage the ex-partner feels towards the step-parent, both as a lover and as a new parent to her child.

* The jealousy the step-parent feels towards the lover's ex-partner and children.

* The guilt the absent parent feels towards the children he has deserted.

* The rivalry between the step-parent and the stepchild for the attention of the new partner/parent.

* Unresolved conflict with past partners.

* Inadequate mourning following the death of a partner/parent.

* The rivalry between half- and step-siblings.

* The divided loyalty and resentment felt by the extended family.

The jealousy and rage the ex-partner feels towards the step-parent, both as a lover and as a new parent to her child

Jealousy is a hideous emotion. At its most intense it can feel as if the sufferer is literally being attacked with a weapon, the pain is so bad. The intensity of this pain can drive people to all sorts of vicious and vindictive acts – almost anything, from the recent much-publicized act of one wife who cut off all the right sleeves of her husband's vast and expensive collection of suits, to another who dumped gloss paint on her unfaithful partner's new Porsche, to the other end of the spectrum where physical harm, even murder, can take place. Fiction and drama are stuffed with such revenge scenarios.

A more common effect of jealousy is manipulation of any children involved. The injured party will use the child as a weapon to punish the absent parent, making access difficult, pouring poison into the child's ear about the parent and the step-parent, making the child feel guilty about enjoying visits to the deserting parent and new partner, cutting the child off from grandparents, aunts and cousins of the the absent parent. All this is understandable, in fact it would take superhuman control not to express some negativity towards the person, or people, who have caused the pain, but the child is the innocent party in all this and does not need to be involved. He does not need to hear an endless diatribe about a parent he loves and whom, until recently, his other parent has been happy for him to love, especially as the absent parent is not there to defend himself. The child does not need to feel guilty or to lie about wanting and enjoying contact with the absent parent or his family. He does not need to be turned against the new step-parent. Neither does he need his parent pretending the negativity does not exist; the child will not believe this denial either, and will be bewildered by it.

It is possible, however, for a parent to admit to her child that she is angry, but to explain that the anger is strictly between the adults involved and nothing to do with the child or the child's behaviour. It is perhaps unrealistic to expect a person to like their child's new step-parent, but for the sake of the child's happiness an attempt should be made not to voice a negative opinion to the child, and, at the very least, to encourage parental contact. If a parent has any real concerns regarding the care their child is receiving from his step-parent, the matter should be taken up directly with the ex-partner, not with the child.

Claire was so distraught when Dominic left that all she wanted was to erase him completely from her life, and that meant her daughter's life too:

> I genuinely convinced myself at the time that it would
> be better for Stephanie, then aged nine, if she never saw
> her father and his new girlfriend again. I deliberately
> moved miles away and whenever Dominic rang to speak to
> Steffi I would make some excuse about her being out, or

ill, or asleep. Then I changed my phone number without telling him and refused to answer the letters he wrote. He sent Stephanie a bicycle for her birthday, but I hid it and never allowed her to see it, then quickly sold it. Whenever Steffi asked questions about her father, I told her he was away on business and too busy to remember us . . . he always had been in the past.

Dominic finally sent a solicitor's letter saying that if he was not allowed access to his daughter he would take me to court. I ignored it, but before he had the chance to try Steffi herself brought things to a head. The day after her eleventh birthday, when I had again destroyed the birthday card and money Dominic had sent her, Steffi ran away. She had a ballet lesson after school, and apparently she primed her friend to tell the teacher she had a bad ankle and wouldn't be in class, and told me she was staying overnight with her friend, something she often did after ballet. So it wasn't until the police rang at midnight that I had any notion there was anything wrong. Steffi had been picked up, upset but unharmed, wandering about the town centre where we had lived before the divorce.

I remember a moment of blind panic, then the absolute certainty dawning that Steffi had gone in search of her father, and knowing too in that moment how wrong I had been to deny her and Dominic access to each other. Steffi had been extremely distraught on her birthday when she hadn't got a card from her father yet again, and I think I began to realize then, for the first time, the pain she'd been going through. I made the mistake of thinking that because Steffi so seldom asked about him she didn't miss him, but the fact was I'd made it impossible for her by flying off the handle and bursting into tears every time his name was mentioned, and I think she was terrified to set me off.

The police insisted they seek professional help to resolve the situation between them, but Claire and Dominic came to an arrangement by themselves which meant Stephanie could go to her father whenever she chose. The sad fact is that vital years of Stephanie's childhood had been lost in the wrangling and she never felt quite at ease with her father and his new family. Claire is horrified now that she was responsible for allowing her quite understandable jealousy to have such a far-reaching and detrimental effect on her daughter.

The jealousy the step-parent feels towards his lover's ex-partner and children

This, you could say, goes with the territory. When someone takes on a person who is still in, or has just come out of, a long relationship where children are involved, they have to live with the fact of that first family, and if they can't they should not take that person on.

One of the problems is the fear that their partner will return to the first family; it happens often enough. Another is resentment of the closeness engendered by children, but, as discussed earlier, parents are for life. One stepmother says that her husband still has his ex-wife's front-door key even twelve years after the separation, so he can drop in on the children whenever he wants to. At the start of their relationship she remembers doing anything she could to stop him going round there: tears, sex, a row, his favourite food, and when he finally did go she would be a nervous wreck until he got back. A stepfather complained of the irritating mutual pride his stepchild's parents took in the child's achievement at the school sports day, which he felt brought them uncomfortably close and excluded him. Another step-parent remembers crying when she gave birth to her daughter because it was not a new experience for her husband as well (he had two children already).

There is no cure for this painful and often irrational jealousy, except to see it for what it is, but there is no reason for it to concern anyone else, except if a step-parent's jealousy means she actually goes to lengths to keep the absent parent away from his first family, as in the first example. Obviously a parent has the ultimate responsibility for seeing his child after separation, but the attitude of a step-parent can be key to making that relationship as easy as possible. Even the most committed of parents will quail at the prospect of seeing their child when every time they make the effort they are faced with tantrums and strife from their current partner. With such a large percentage of separated fathers losing touch with their children within two years, and an even larger percentage within five years, it is clear that the absent parent needs all the help available to make sure the child is in touch with both his parents throughout childhood.

The guilt the absent parent feels towards the children he has deserted

Shock at the intensity of the pain and guilt parents can feel when they leave the family home is very common. You might say it is obvious that a parent would suffer in this situation, but so often the conflict two adults undergo in the break-up of a relationship sidelines the children until much later. One father's testimony related:

> If I had known the pain and guilt I would still be feeling, even ten years after the split, I think I might not have left, but at the time I had such an appalling relationship with their mother and I thought, 'Oh, I'll work it out with the kids later.' I knew we loved each other and I knew my wife wouldn't make it difficult for me to see them, but once I left it was never the same. I see them a lot, we live nearby, and it is getting better now they are older, but there is none of that relaxed closeness you get when you live with a child every day. With each visit we have to

sort of remake our closeness. My wife has forgiven me, whatever that means, and I've apologized to the kids, but the guilt remains; it always will, I suppose.

With some parents this guilt makes them try to overcompensate their children with limitless treats and presents. This is unnecessary. All a child requires is love and commitment, sometimes the hardest thing to give at a distance, but whereas endless material compensation might buy the child's attention in the short term, it won't buy love and respect. Step-parents also resent the vast financial outpourings which are the result of this guilt, especially if there is noticeable discrimination as regards the new family.

The rivalry between the step-parent and the stepchild for the attention of the new partner/parent

It is hard, especially for someone with no children of their own, to understand the parenting relationship and the importance parents quite rightly attach to the happiness of their children. It is hard to accommodate strange children, perhaps to have to give up a cosy evening because the child won't sleep, to have to forgo a party because there is no babysitter, to be unable to have a sensible conversation, or sex, because of childish interruptions. These are all things a parent gets used to over a period of time, having a vested interest in the child; a step-parent has to adjust much more quickly.

Most step-parents feel guilty for being jealous. One man said:

> I understood in my head that she loved the boy and had to put him first (he was only five at the time), I would have thought less of her if she hadn't, but sometimes when she would give him attention instead of me I would feel insanely jealous, almost as if he was another lover.

41

I would sulk like a big kid. It made me feel as if I was really sick in the head but I couldn't explain to her how I felt because it was so bloody childish. In the end it didn't work out for us.

Jealousy is often the result of insecurity – 'She loves him more than me' – which an adult sees as ridiculous in relation to a child, but someone who has never had a child of their own cannot necessarily understand the intensity of parental love and how exclusive it can seem to an outsider. However ridiculous this man felt his jealousy to be, it was quite understandable, and if only he could have explained to his new partner how he felt they might have had a chance of working it out. It is also important for each group to have time alone. A child needs time with his parent without the constraints of an unfamiliar adult, the adults need time away from the child (as parents in a conventional family do) to cement their own relationship, and the stepchild and step-parent need time together to get to know one another.

A child's jealousy is more straightforward, without the added pressure of guilt. All children want their parents' unlimited attention, but most children learn that this is not possible. After a separation a child may actually get the undivided attention of the resident parent for a while, and any person who intrudes too quickly on this relationship without giving the child time to adjust will immediately be the object of jealous rivalry. It is also true that children may have become used to a physically undemonstrative relationship between their parents and find the sexual intensity of a new relationship confusing and jealous-making. As with the step-parent, gradual acclimatization to the new situation and plenty of time apart can make the stepchild's acceptance of the step-parent much more likely.

Jenny remembers her mother having a rule when her stepfather first came to live with them. Every Saturday afternoon, no matter what was going on, she and her mother would go out together somewhere, the park, swimming, a pizza, the cinema. Her mother would joke to Danny, Jenny's stepfather: 'No, you can't come, no matter how much you want to, this is our time, go away.' Jenny remembers feeling very special when her mother said this and she would always look forward to the time, not because of what they actually did, or because she had her mother's exclusive attention, but because her mother had acknowledged Jenny's importance in the new relationship. She says it also taught her to tolerate the time her mother had with Danny from which she was excluded. It is a measure of the success of this ploy that after a while Jenny actually wanted Danny to come with them on the Saturday outings.

Unresolved conflict with past partners

A large area of difficulty in a stepfamily is the unresolved conflict from the previous relationship. It is not surprising that most people who have been involved in a marriage with children do not give up that marriage lightly, and when they do there is often a great deal of pain, bitterness and a terrible sense of failure which is sometimes never confronted, sometimes never even discussed, before the two adults immerse themselves in new relationships, carrying with them the baggage from the old one. The dangers of this lack of resolution cannot be over-emphasized.

Martha had been married to Eric for ten years when she found him in bed with another parent on the PTA. This was the fourth time she had been faced with his infidelity, but this time was the last and she threw him out. Before and after he left she tried to understand what had made him do it; she says she could have forgiven a 'once off', but he refused to discuss it with her, so she blamed herself, thinking it was because she was not sexy or attractive enough to hold on to him. Along with the sense of failure and blame she carried away was a plummeting self-esteem.

Quite a while later she began a relationship with Max. He was quite unlike her husband in many ways, but she soon found herself convinced that he would go the way of Eric and be unfaithful to her.

She says it began to obsess her; she would open his mail, check the phone bill, search his pockets, ring him at restaurants where he said he was having lunch. Then one day she found herself following him to a friend's house and sitting outside in the dark watching the window, waiting for him to show himself with another woman. She broke the relationship off soon after because she felt she would rather be alone than be prey to this jealousy and suspicion, despite the fact that otherwise he was a good stepfather and a good partner.

When she went for counselling in an attempt to understand the jealousy, the counsellor suggested she contact Eric and talk it out with him. Although this surprised her, so long after the split, she agreed, and so did Eric, which surprised her even more. He admitted his infidelity was nothing to do with her, that he had always found her attractive, but that it was a compulsion which had continued into his present relationship and was already causing trouble, and he didn't understand it either. Once she realized that it had been Eric's problem not hers, and that she had allowed it to become her problem, she felt much less insecure and eventually mended her fences with Max.

It is also common for the bitterness and jealousies of the previous relationship to become an unfortunate ritual of the new one. It is not easy for a new family to live happily with a parent or partner who is forever rowing violently down the phone or on the door-step with her ex-partner, or spends each meal-time carping and criticizing the ex-partner's behaviour or reminiscing about all the iniquities of her previous relationship, however much they might sympathize. These are things that should be resolved to a manageable degree by the time a new relationship is embarked upon. No one is asking a person to forget what happened, no one is asking them never to refer to it, no one is asking that they don't have the occasional row with their 'ex', and certainly no one is asking that they like them, but it is important for anyone who separates to make time to resolve the main differences and come to some mutual understanding about how they will relate to each other and their children in the future. Even if both sides agree to dislike each other for the rest of time it's some sort of agreement!

Inadequate mourning following the death of a partner/parent

Argument and bitterness hanging over from a previous relationship are an obvious problem for the stepfamily; a less obvious one is bringing the dead partner into the new relationship because of unresolved grieving. The British, it could be said, are generally not good at dealing with their emotions, and death is a spectacular example of this. Also the increasingly secular nature of our modern society removes the comfort that religious ritual might have offered in the past. So when a parent dies it is not uncommon for the child to be completely excluded from the funeral service, and encouraged to carry on as if nothing has happened. The surviving parent does this from understandable, if misguided, motives, i.e.: 'He's much too young to understand, the coffin will only upset him.' This is true, the coffin will upset him, but he must be allowed to say goodbye to his parent if he wants to, he must be allowed to ask questions, he must be allowed to keep his parent in his memory without fear of reproach, his insecurity at the loss of his parent must be addressed.

If he is not given this opportunity then there is a danger of fantasy and myth growing up around the dead parent. He may not believe his parent is actually dead because it hasn't been explained properly: 'Daddy had to go away,' 'Daddy has gone to a better place and we won't be seeing him any more,' 'Mummy didn't want to go, but God wanted her because she was such a good person,' euphemisms that are lost on a child. He may put his dead parent on a pedestal, encouraged to do so by the remaining parent. This parent may not be able to cope with her own grief, and may also retain feelings of anger and loss. None of this will be easy for an incoming step-parent to deal with. Living under the shadow of a 'perfect' husband, a 'perfect' marriage and a 'perfect' father, he risks not being given the chance to measure up and his presence could be very much resented by his stepchild, his behaviour constantly compared unfavourably to his predecessor by both partner and stepchild.

A parent should not be afraid of sharing her grief. She should allow the family to be together and support each other and not make light of the funeral process. It is important to talk about the dead person lovingly but realistically and not to exclude the children from this process It is only when a person has had time to mourn properly that she will be able to move on without taking unnecessary baggage into another relationship.

Judy was nine when her father died suddenly of a heart attack:

> It happened early in the morning. Mummy came into our bedroom and said, 'Daddy is dead . . .' then left, obviously overcome and worried about showing it. After that she never talked about him again. We were taken to Richmond Park for a walk that morning, and then I had to do my homework. I remember I had to learn a poem and the next day I stood up and recited it, word perfect. As I was doing it I remember thinking: 'Nothing will ever be the same again . . . I am different from all these girls and they don't know it.' No one had said anything to me, the teacher never even acknowledged what had happened to me, I wasn't told about the funeral, though my sister went, and we never dared speak about Daddy because Mum would start to cry. It was as if I had never had a father. We both grew up thinking he and Mum had a perfect marriage and that he had been perfect, not from anything she said, but from what she didn't say. When I married I was terrified my husband would die at any moment, and when we had arguments I thought our marriage must be a failure

because it wasn't perfect like Mum and Dad's. I never
found out if they had problems, even as a mature adult
I didn't dare ask my mother about him.

The rivalry between half- and step-siblings

A degree of sibling rivalry is common amongst all children, but
when rivalry becomes a problem it is almost always because it has
been exacerbated by parental or step-parental behaviour. There is
an enormous reservoir of distress from stepchildren about the
unfair treatment parents and step-parents mete out to stepchildren
compared to that meted out to their half-siblings. This distress
can arise from perceived financial disadvantage, general material
disadvantage, room-space disadvantage and parent-time disadvantage which takes the form of being singled out for disapproval,
dislike and exclusion after the birth of the half-sibling.

*Tasha had a stepfather and two half-siblings. She says that in the
evenings when the family were all sitting watching television her
stepfather would say: 'Go to your room, we don't want you down
here with us,' and her mother would say nothing in her support.
She says she would go upstairs and tidy her room obsessively, and
even to this day, when she's upset, she goes and does the same
thing. She says she was so jealous of her brothers that she would
cheerfully have killed them. No matter what they did, they got away
with it, but if she did the same thing they would be down on her
like a ton of bricks. Luckily she went to live with her father when
she was ten, so she escaped further damage.*

Another example:

*Rene's parents divorced when she was barely one. She lived first
with her mother, then with her father, each of whom had two more
children. One day, aged twenty, she had a call from her mother:
'Rene, I was just doing my will and I wanted you to know that I'm*

*not leaving you anything, I'm leaving it to the other two, because
I assume your father will have left you something, and the others
have only got me. I'm sure you'll understand.'*

*Rene, needless to say, did not understand and was truly hurt by
her mother's action.*

These are extreme examples, but every degree exists. Of course,
once a child has been made aware of inequalities, he will always be
on the lookout for them, and can end up perceiving unfairness
where there is, in fact, none. It is easy to see how these inequalities
arise if parents are not aware of the likelihood. A step-parent comes
into a family with no parenting experience and is faced with a
stepchild. Even if he gets on well with that child it will still initially
be a friendship rather than a relationship; after all, the child has a
father, whether he is dead or alive, part of his life or not. A few years
on, or perhaps sooner, he and his partner have a child of their own.
This child is their child, the product of their relationship, there
is no other man down the road to cause rifts or divided loyalties,
this child is his and he feels like a father for the first time. But,
whereas it is only sensible to admit that he *feels* differently about
his own child, it is not either sensible or fair to treat his own child
and his stepchild differently. (Later chapters discuss this more fully.)
If he does, and the child's parent lets him, it is hardly surprising if
they engender sibling rivalry in their various offspring.

The divided loyalty and resentment
felt by the extended family

Most children grow up with some contact, often a great deal of
contact, with the extended family of one, or both, parents. When a
couple separate it is very hard for this extended family, who are
probably only hearing one side of the story, to know how to behave,
whom to support and whether they can remain impartial or not.

The 'Well, of course, I never trusted her' syndrome is unfortunately only too common. Whereas the family can be a great support

to a separated parent and his children, they can also cause problems by promoting resentment and blame with regard to the ex-partner, criticizing her parenting, dredging up grudges from the past, none of which is at all helpful to their relative, however much they might think this is a form of support.

The 'Well, of course, Janet used to be so much better at ...' syndrome is the other side of the same coin when a family have been very close to a relative's spouse and then resent any new partner who comes on the scene, isolating the stepfamily from the important relationship with the extended family.

It is understandable for a parent wanting to put the past behind him to be reluctant to be in contact with his ex-partner's family, and for the extended family to back up his decision from a sense of loyalty, but if the children have been close to a maternal grandparent or perhaps an aunt, it is unfair to add to the child's sense of loss by preventing contact with these hopefully impartial sources of comfort. Many parents fail to realize just how isolated a child can feel after a separation or divorce.

David has always been glad that he kept in contact with his wife's mother, Susan, after their very acrimonious divorce. Susan often had his daughter, Amy, to stay in their house by the sea and he says she always knew when Amy had something that was bothering her because she would say: 'Let's go for a walk on the beach, Grandma.'

One day Amy poured out her problems with her stepfather, which were already in the category of mental abuse. She said she had tried to talk to her mother about him but that her mother had been angry and told Amy it was her fault if they didn't get on because she didn't make enough effort with her stepfather. She hadn't dared tell her father because she was frightened of what he might do.

Susan told Amy she would talk to her parents about the situation, and much to the child's relief she was sent to live with her father. David and Susan both doubt that Amy would have spoken at all if she hadn't been aware that her grandmother could act as an intermediary with both of her parents.

To summarize:

By identifying the possible areas of conflict in a stepfamily it is possible to accept that they are normal. By accepting that they are normal they can then be discussed, and solutions can be found that work for your particular stepfamily. The problems above are all discussed at greater length in the subsequent chapters, but here are a few pointers to be getting on with:

* Help your partner keep any ongoing conflict with an ex-partner away from the children.

* If you decide to be involved with someone who already has a family then you must accept the importance of that family. If you can't, then get out.

* Don't allow guilt from your partner's separation to affect the way you both parent your child ... no one benefits from excessive spoiling.

* Accept that jealousies in the early stages of a stepfamily are probably inevitable. Give everyone time to adjust.

* Help your partner to resolve the pain and conflict from her previous relationship as much as possible before embarking on a stepfamily. This includes the grief and loss when a partner dies.

* Treat all half-siblings, step-siblings and birth-siblings the same in all respects.

* Encourage your partner to maintain contact with the members of her ex-partner's family with whom the children are close. A beloved granny can be very comforting.

* You might despair of things ever settling down, but with care and consideration I assure you ... it can work.

CHAPTER 4

The part-time stepfamily

The part-time stepfamily is both easier in some ways than the full-time stepfamily, but also more difficult. It is easier in that the part-time parent and step-parent have none of the day-to-day responsibility which full-time parenting involves, such as the boring homework slog, the school runs, the washing. If there is friction between the child and the step-parent, then it can be arranged that they have little contact on the child's visits, but if they get on well the step-parent can afford to be relaxed with the child, freed from the burden of normal parental responsibility.

The part-time stepfamily can be more difficult in that the step-parent never has enough normal day-to-day contact with her stepchild to really get to know the child well and forge a close relationship, and the parent can find himself losing touch with his child without the daily contact the resident parent enjoys. When children visit their parents on a part-time basis a great deal of adjustment has to take place for everyone, but particularly for the child.

Easing the way for the child

The child has to fit into another family which is both her family and not her family. Each time she visits she must somehow make a space for herself where she can feel 'at home', even if it is for only one night a week, and may perhaps have to forgo parties and events with her friends at home. There are many things a parent and step-parent can do to ease the path for their child:

* **Encourage your partner not to fight with her ex-partner in front of the children.** This can never be over-emphasized. No child is helped by two warring parents. Imagine being the child in this scenario:

Letty, aged six, hears the front-door bell ring. She is thrilled because she knows it is her father. She is too small to reach the latch, but her mother pretends she hasn't heard and goes on ironing angrily, banging the iron back and forth on Letty's T-shirt. Letty is terrified her father will go away again.

'Mum, Mum, it's Dad . . . Dad's at the door.'

Her mother nonchalantly stops ironing.

'Really? Well, let him wait,' she replies, her voice full of hatred.

Letty grabs her hand.

'Please, Mum . . . please, open the door. He'll think we aren't here.'

Eventually Mum opens the door and stands, arms crossed, glaring at her ex-husband. He is looking worried and sheepish.

'Hello, Gloria . . . everything OK?'

Gloria snorts. 'Oh yeah, just fine.' Letty's father does not even greet his daughter, he is too wrapped up in the anger between himself and his ex-wife.

'If that woman's going to be there then Letty's not coming,' Gloria snaps.

'She isn't, we agreed, didn't we? Don't you trust me?'

This is a stupid thing to say. Of course Gloria doesn't trust him and he brings an angry tirade down on his head which he pretends to ignore.

'Hello, sweetheart.' He finally kisses his daughter.

'What woman?' Letty asks, bewildered.

'You see?' Her father hisses at Gloria.

'And I want her back tonight by seven.'

'But you said she could stay the night.' Her father looks crestfallen.

'Well, she can't. If you're going to make a fuss she won't come at all.'

'You have to let me see her, it's the law . . . Letty, you want to stay the night with me, don't you?'

Letty looks from one parent to the other. Both are glaring at her and she's sure she's done something wrong but doesn't know what. She does want to stay, but she's frightened of what her mother will do if she says so. She begins to cry.

'Now look what you've done.' Gloria spits, gathering Letty in her arms. Letty struggles out and her father grabs her arm and begins dragging her off down the path. Her mother begins to cry.

'You bastard,' she shouts at Letty's father. 'You bloody bastard. Bring her back tonight, she can't stay, bring her back,' she sobs so the whole neighbourhood can hear.

Letty's father says in the car: 'You do want to stay, don't you, sweetheart? We had such fun last time, didn't we?'

Letty just shakes her head miserably. She no longer knows what she wants except that her parents be pleasant to each other.

This may seem like an extreme scenario but degrees of it are, unfortunately, played out regularly over the issue of children's visiting arrangements. As a step-parent you can help your partner by discussing the best plan of action for the child and supporting him without getting directly involved. When your partner makes an arrangement it should be stuck to and the child informed of the plan in advance. Although it is the responsibility of a parent to make arrangements to see his own child, a step-parent can be very influential in either obstructing or facilitating this process.

* **Make a proper space for your stepchild in your new home.**
This is essential, especially when there are half-siblings involved. No child can feel at home when they have no proper bed or their toys are moved and spoilt by the other children when they are absent. It is not always easy because of the constraints of space, but make some place, even if it's a corner of a bedroom,

a cupboard, a special drawer, where a visiting child can keep his own things and know that they will not be touched by anyone between visits.

Jessica stayed with her father only once a month, but she remembers he made a corner of the playroom hers with a desk, chair and toy-box. Her two half-siblings were smaller than her but were kept strictly away, and when she arrived she always went straight to her corner and looked at all her toys. She says now that she thinks it gave her time to orientate herself and feel that she belonged and was respected by her father's second family. Also it made her feel a bit special, different to her half-siblings, but different in a good way.

* **Decide between you *beforehand* how the visiting child will be disciplined.** It is essential not to discriminate as regards discipline between a visiting child and any resident half- or step-siblings. This can be a major source of resentment, so agree that the visiting child will be disciplined exactly the same as any resident children. There is a tendency to spoil the visiting child, but the child in question does not appreciate this, nor do any half-siblings. Likewise he does not appreciate being made the scapegoat for all the bad behaviour of his half-siblings.

Harry and his half-sister Claire were messing about where they had been told specifically not to and broke a valuable lamp. Harry's step-mother yelled at Claire and sent her to her room, but Harry was let off 'because he is only visiting'. Harry was devastated and burst into tears: 'Why don't you shout at me like you do at the others?' he wailed to his stepmother. His stepmother had only been trying to be kind to him in the short time he was with them.

* **Decide with your stepchild what you, as a step-parent, will be called.** The child can be involved in this decision. 'Mum' or 'Dad' is not a good idea. The child already has one of each and is only visiting for short periods. There are situations with full-time step-parenting when this can be acceptable, but this is discussed in the next chapter.

* **Offer time alone.** Give the visiting child the choice of time alone with his parent if he wants it. However, he might prefer to be treated as part of the gang.

* **Explain the 'house rules'.** Let the child know about the basic 'house rules', which may be quite different to those he has at home. At home he may be allowed to eat his food with his fingers and stay up till midnight. Don't expect him to change immediately, but explain that you do things differently. This is better than yelling at him for not instantly understanding and conforming to your way of life, and better than saying nothing and allowing tension to build up with what you see as unsociable behaviour. An explanation could go like this, and might come better from the parent than from the step-parent: 'I realize that Mum lets you eat with your fingers, and that's fine, but when you're here I'd rather you used a fork because I'm a bit fussy that way.'
  Don't allow yourself, as a step-parent, to be blamed.

* **Don't allow your partner or yourself to put pressure on your visiting stepchild to have non-stop *fun*.** It is understandable for a parent who sees his child only for a limited period to want that short time to be special, but this is unfair to the child. The child just wants to be with the parent they miss in the same way they used to when the parent was still resident. Endless outings and gifts just confuse and upset them.

Isabelle, seven at the time, remembers weekends with her father as a non-stop jamboree of Hamley's toy-shop, Macdonald's, Madame Tussaud's, the Planetarium, museums, funfairs and theatres. The presents he bought her irritated her mother so much that she dreaded taking them home and would 'accidentally' forget to, which in turn upset her father. It wasn't until she actually vomited one weekend in Hamley's from nerves and exhaustion that her father stopped for long enough to listen and find out that all she really wanted was for them to hang out together at his flat.

This is also true of holidays. Many part-time parents try to create the perfect holiday with endless fun and frolics, and require non-stop smiles, happiness and gratitude in return. This expectation is doomed and will result in sulky children and frustrated, angry parents. Try to relax and enjoy just being together.

* **Be fair, financially, materially and with your time.** When children are only visiting for short periods it is easy to spoil them with presents like Isabelle's well-intentioned father did, but the flip side is when the resident children seem to have all the advantages and the visiting child feels left out and becomes jealous. One adult stepchild is still aggrieved twenty years on:

> We visited Dad almost every weekend. Mum was one of
> those people who never bothered to organize any-
> thing, but our stepmother was the exact opposite and
> our half-brother and sister had piano lessons, swimming
> lessons, and, the real bone of contention, a pony each.
> I loved riding and I was sometimes allowed a ride at week-
> ends if the others weren't eventing or whatever, which
> they practically always were, but when I asked for my own
> pony I was told it wouldn't be sensible because I didn't
> live there. I understand now that perhaps it would have
> been impractical, but I also realize that that wasn't the real
> problem, the real problem was that my stepmother was
> so engrossed in the others she didn't want to include me
> and my sister, even for two days a week, and I really hated
> her for that. I felt we were second best and my father
> did nothing to support us. I think they both thought,
> Oh, don't worry, they'll be gone on Sunday . . . and
> of course we were.

Sandra's parents, on the other hand, managed it better:

> I was lucky because we lived close and I could come and go
> between my parents whenever I pleased. I felt I had an
> advantage having two homes and two families rather than
> the reverse. I had a bedroom in each and clothes in each

and my parents and step-parents were cool about where I was as long as I told them. It was great because when stuff was going on I didn't fancy, like dinner parties or housework, I used to escape to the other place. It got me into trouble sometimes, but I think I had much more variety in my childhood and I certainly argued less with both my parents when I was a teenager than most of my friends, because I knew I didn't have to be there all the time and they knew it too. I think I felt sort of superior in some ways to my half-brothers and sisters (she had a half-brother in one family, two half-sisters in the other). I remember one day Jason, my little half-brother, wanted to come back with me to my mother's house because he assumed Mum's house must be his other home in the same way it was mine. He cried when my stepmother said he couldn't.

* **Be flexible about visits.** Step-parents and parents should let the child know that she can be flexible with her visits to them and not be hurt if there is a friend's party she wants to go to one weekend instead of visiting them. Another arrangement can be made which suits everyone. This is particularly true when the child gets into teenage and is old enough to come and go independently.

Easing the way for the part-time parent

The parent who sees his child only at weekends has adjustments to make too. He may not feel so at ease with his child any more and may feel that he does not know him as he used to, he may still feel guilty about the problems the separation has caused his child, he may feel the child is an unfortunate reminder of his previous partner. He must make room in his new life for his first family, but only for limited periods of time, and must somehow maintain a satisfactory relationship with his first children on this less than satisfactory basis. A step-parent can help her partner by understanding how he might be feeling.

He misses the closeness

Families are built gradually on the familiarity of day-to-day closeness, sharing moments as they happen, getting used to each other's habits, good and bad, talking out problems together, and it is this family intimacy, which most people take for granted, that the absent parent (usually the father) has to forgo when separation or divorce takes place.

It is not easy seeing a child on a part-time basis and it is not altogether surprising that a large percentage of fathers lose touch with their children in the first few years after separation. If a parent continues to live close to his family then maintaining the casual nature of short, unplanned visits such as popping in after school can be maintained, but often families are separated geographically too and when the children are still small the visits have to be much more structured and formal. This means the absent parent has to make a special effort to keep up with the daily life of his child if he is to maintain a close relationship throughout his childhood, and his new partner can be a great help in this by recognizing the importance of this relationship, being supportive, and not standing in the way of the practical considerations, such as:

> ✳ If possible it is advisable to stay geographically close to the parent's first family. This may seem like a bad idea when a couple have been involved in an acrimonious split – instinct might tell them to flee in opposite directions – but it will make things more difficult for everyone if they do.

> ✳ If a parent cannot be geographically close then it is a good idea for him to telephone the child often. A step-parent needs to make it easy for his partner to fix a regular

time to do this which is convenient to all parties. The call need not be long and dramatic, frequent short calls are better, especially when the child is small. Letters and postcards should also be encouraged between parent and child.

* Visiting arrangements are best kept as flexible as is practical. Obviously thoughtless disruptions are not good for a child, but it should be possible to legislate for the odd spontaneous visit between the families.

* A parent should try to make realistic arrangements he can stick to, and a step-parent can help facilitate this by supporting her partner and not being obstructive.

* Both parent and step-parent can make sure that when the child visits they leave enough time when things are not going on and other people are not present to talk and exchange thoughts. A step-parent has to be sensitive about how much of this time the child needs alone with his parent.

* Important events in a child's life are not limited to birthday and Christmas. It is easy to remember birthdays, but neither parent nor step-parent should forget the violin exam, the football match, the school trip, etc. All children want to tell their parents about these events.

* A child always wants his parent to turn up to school open days, plays, carol services, important sports events, etc. If it's impossible then a parent should phone and find out how it went.

* Many absent parents lose touch with their child's progress at school because they are not included in invitations to parents' evenings, exam decisions and school events. Schools are happy to send duplicate reports and invitations if requested.

He feels guilty

However pointless this may seem to a new partner, most part-time parents feel this. Separation and divorce are unpleasant, everyone would agree about that, but if a person has thought long and hard about it and decided there is no other solution, then he must try to put this guilt behind him. If he doesn't then it may colour the way he feels about his children and could affect his relationship with them for ever. All a parent can do is to apologize to his children and continue to support them as much as he can. He must accept that they might be angry at first, but that anger will be mitigated if he stands by them and they can be secure in the fact that they haven't lost him as a parent.

Maria was fifteen when her father ran off with another woman.

> I was furious with him, jealous and frightened I might never see him again. If he'd avoided the issue then I doubt I'd be speaking to him now, but he faced up to my anger, let me be angry, apologized and tried to explain, but didn't try to excuse what he'd done. While I was furious, I still admired him for being brave enough to do that; it can't have been easy confronting me, knowing how much I would be hurt. I said I didn't want to meet the woman (I think I called her 'that bitch'), and he went along with that for ages, although I knew he was dying to introduce us. Obviously I wish it hadn't happened, but Mum and Dad are both happier now I think and even my stepmum is quite cool.

If a parent doesn't deal with the guilt then he is in danger of associating that guilt with his child and in the end will be inclined to avoid her.

Frank fell into a depression when he separated from his wife and had to leave his children.

> I just never realized how dreadful it would be not seeing them all the time and when I did see them it was always so

tense and difficult because I didn't have anywhere proper to live and we had to meet in cafés and the park. I couldn't get it out of my head that I'd ruined their lives. When Mikey failed his exams I knew it was my fault . . . it was hell and I began to avoid seeing them, it seemed easier to just run away than to see them like this and be reminded what a mess I'd made of things. It wasn't until I got ill, I mean depressed ill, that things changed. Sharon, my ex, got in touch and said how worried the boys were and how they missed me and how they wanted to see me. It seems daft now, but I was actually surprised. I thought, 'Why do they want to see a worthless old bugger like me?' Thank God it worked out. I don't like talking about emotional stuff, men don't, but me and the boys did talk after a fashion and I realized they missed me and that, whatever I'd done, I was still their dad.

He feels he has no influence with his children

Part of being a parent is having influence over your children's lives, and one of the things that a part-time parent finds very difficult is a reduction in this influence:

John's two children stayed with their mother after a bitter divorce and John initially wanted nothing to do with his ex-wife. He saw his children once a month on arranged visits, but had no contact with his wife except the most basic information, pick-up times, for example:

It never occurred to me that she would change the children's lives without reference to me until one day Tammy, my daughter, who was then aged eleven, rang to say she was starting at a boarding-school in September. I was horrified, this had been a massive bone of contention between me and Helen, I'd been to boarding-school and loathed it, but she was always very keen for both the children to go. I suppose I should have thought she'd do something like this, but I was still living in the past a bit, I didn't realize how little I had come to know about my children's lives and how little influence I now had over their future.

He rang up in a rage, but there was nothing he could do at that stage, and because he had such a bad relationship with Helen he had no basis even for a discussion. This made him think hard, and gradually, over the next few months, gritting his teeth initially, he began to mend his fences with her, realizing that if he didn't do something now he would have no say at all in the future education of his children, or in any other area either. He arranged to see the school and asked for reports and information to be sent to him as well as his wife, and from then on he attended all the functions and open days. Helen was very hostile at first, but gradually, although too much had been said for them ever to be friends, they did manage to establish a working relationship with regard to the children which allowed him some say in their lives.

The decision about boarding-school was an important one, but it can be just as frustrating for a parent to watch his child eating badly or listen to her using swear words he has forbidden, taking attitudes he doesn't approve of or having freedoms he considers dangerous. Sometimes there is nothing he can do about this except let the child know how he is feeling, but a good, established dialogue with the resident parent at least gives him the chance to try.

His child is a reminder of his ex-partner

The parent with whom a child resides will inevitably pass on habits, speech patterns and attitudes to the child. If she is the same sex the child might even resemble her mother in her choice of dress, a son his father. Many part-time parents seeing their children on weekend visits can find this similarity either painful or irritating and may unfairly pass this on to the child.

'Mum was a regular hippy,' Tracey remembers with a wry smile.

> She ran off with my stepfather, who was also a hippy, and they sort of hippy'd away in Lincolnshire. I thought this was normal when I was small, and when I went to stay with Dad, who lived in Manchester and worked in insurance, I used to rant on about organic vegetables and dolphin-friendly tuna and Dad used to get furious. Then one day, when I was about fourteen, I turned up in a sort of flowy Indian cotton dress with a nose-stud! This was in the eighties when everyone was smart and mean. Dad went ballistic and refused to take me out unless I removed the stud, which I wouldn't, and we had an almighty row. He was quite straight, my dad, but I was surprised he was so upset by a little nose-stud. When he calmed down we talked and he eventually explained: 'You look lovely, and the nose-stud is fine if that's your thing, but all this hippy stuff just reminds me so much of your mother, and you even look like her now, like she did when we first fell in love . . . I just find it hard to cope with.'

These similarities and comparisons are inevitable, but most children are very much themselves whatever their influences, and it's best to appreciate the differences and not dwell on the things that cannot be changed, or feel guilty for noticing them.

He dreads family festivities such as Christmas

Festivities such as Christmas cause problems for a large proportion of the population who have awkward family relationships, but for none more so than the stepfamily. Obviously parents want to be with their children over Christmas, and children with their parents, and when this is not possible a lot of grief and conflict can be created. If you live close to your separated family this won't be such a problem, but if you are geographically distant it is best to make plans for each parent to take alternate years. This way everyone knows where they stand, and it is usually possible to make the days around the festivities available to the other parent.

The part-time step-parent's perspective

The part-time step-parent has to be willing to allow a child she perhaps hardly knows to come in and out of her family and her life for short periods and to find a role for herself with that child that is acceptable to everyone. Although she is now closely attached to her stepchild she might never really have the chance to get to know him well or have any real say in his life. This situation raises certain questions in the step-parent's mind:

'What is my role?'

It is very hard to establish a meaningful role when a step-parent only sees her stepchild intermittently. As a result, many part-time step-parents opt out altogether and leave the care and disciplining on visits to the parent. This is a mistake, particularly if there are other children involved. It implies that there is something unacceptable about the step-relationship which ought to be avoided and only serves to set up long-term and unnecessary resentment. It is best for a step-parent and parent to discuss right at the outset how they intend to parent the child, then support each other in the decision, especially in matters of discipline, so that the child knows where he stands. Otherwise this kind of scenario can develop:

Suzy was Benny's stepmother and Guy and Andrea's mother. Benny visited every other weekend, and Bill, the children's father, who was still feeling guilty about the divorce, determined that he and he alone would be responsible for Benny's discipline:

> Poor little chap, he's had a difficult time and I only see him twice a month. I want him to have a good time when

he's with me. He won't like it if you tell him what to do
and anyway he gets enough nagging from his mother.
It's better if you let me deal with him.

*This edict from her partner made Suzy dread Benny's visits; he was
a difficult boy and the house would descend into chaos as soon as
he pitched up because he would do exactly what he liked and breed
rebellion in Guy and Andrea too.*

'I just didn't know what to do,' Suzy says.

If they were messing about at table, which they often
did, I think because Benny knew it annoyed me, I would
tell them off. At first the other two would behave, but
Benny would just stare insolently at me and keep on at it,
daring me to say something. If Bill was there he would
say: 'Come on now, Ben, get on with your supper,' not
really telling him off, and Ben would ignore him too!
Of course, as soon as the others, especially Guy, saw that
I couldn't cope, they would side with Benny and start
winding me up again.

I know it sounds pathetic; Benny was a boy of eight or
nine at the time and I was a full-grown, responsible
woman, but he could reduce me to tears quicker than
anyone, although I tried not to let him see that. After a
while I had it out with Bill. I said that if things didn't
change I would just go away on the weekends Benny came
and take the children with me. I think in an odd way
Bill was scared of Benny . . . he'd got so caught up with
the guilt of leaving them, then of course he didn't see him
that much so he didn't really know him. I don't know
what it was, but anyway, he agreed to talk to Benny.
Benny was furious and sulky, but at least I felt I was
entitled to tell him off when he got out of order, and
I certainly did! Strange to say, this helped. As soon as he
knew I meant business and Bill wouldn't protect him,
he calmed down and I think began to respect me a bit.

I don't think either of his parents had ever stood up to him. I can't say we've ever had a great relationship, but we get on OK now and I feel he will at least listen to me.

Parenting is difficult enough not to want to do it alone, and in a stepfamily, whether part- or full-time, it is best to agree to share the parenting of any children in the family, so that the children all know they must accept authority from both parents regardless of their relationship with the adults. This united front is very important in a stepfamily to forge real family closeness, and particularly so in the part-time stepfamily, otherwise separated units are created with one or other member feeling isolated or left out.

'How can I be so jealous of his children?'

The step-parent is often the isolated member of the family in the part-time stepfamily. Most adults feel guilty and inadequate when they realize they are jealous of a child, but this feeling is perfectly natural for a person faced with the intensity and exclusivity of a strong family unit not their own. Unlike the ex-wife or the old girlfriend, children are not going to go away. Many step-parents, particularly part-time ones, are quite happy to accept their stepchildren initially, but when they find they are excluded from the group and that the children are around every weekend, every Christmas and every summer holiday, and the attention they have been receiving from their new partner is suddenly absent at these times, they become less enthusiastic.

Meg's new partner Andy was very close to his three children, then aged thirteen, ten and seven, and saw them every weekend. Meg really liked the children at first but:

They were such a tight unit, they shared the same jokes and of course had a lot of history in common. They were polite, but it wasn't them, it was Andy ... as soon as they arrived every Saturday, Andy just switched off from me. Obviously he didn't want the children to see us kissing or cuddling, and I agreed about that, but they made me feel completely redundant and irrelevant. I don't think it was intentional, they were just very close and Andy always put them first. It meant we never had a proper weekend like normal couples do, and never really had the time to see friends.

It took me a long time to pluck up the courage to say anything to him, and when I did he was horrified that I could admit to being jealous of his children. We argued , but in the end he agreed to try and include me a bit more in the weekends and perhaps have one Saturday a month when they didn't come over. We tried, but it didn't really work out and in the end we split up because I knew the children would always come first for Andy. I think taking on a stepfamily has to be thought out very carefully . . . it's incredibly difficult, but I still feel mean-minded and a failure for not coping better.

What Meg said about taking on a stepfamily is true: if a person finds it impossible to accept the relationship between a new partner and their first family, then it's best for them to bow out early on. However, Andy could have made things much easier for Meg by gradually integrating her into the family and showing the children, by example, that he considered her part of the gang. The children might have been initially resistant, but would eventually have followed their father's lead.

'How can I get to know them better?'

With your resident children, whether or not they are stepchildren, you know what they like to eat, to wear, the sports they enjoy, the crazes they are currently going through, the things they are afraid of. With part-time step-parenting this is not always the case, and the step-parent can feel at a huge disadvantage because of it.

Barbara's partner, Simon, saw his children only very rarely because of geographical distance and financial restraints. When Barbara first

*began living with Simon she worried that she would buy all the
wrong food when they visited but Simon didn't seem to know what
they might eat and refused to ring his ex-wife and ask because he
felt embarrassed that he didn't know. She decided to buy the usual
fish fingers and sausages, chips, beans, the things that children
seem universally to like. They arrived late in the evening on Friday,
both tired from the journey, the boy aged five, the girl seven.
Barbara greeted them and said: 'You must be starving. I've done
fish fingers and sausages, so you can choose, and lots of chips.'*

*Apparently the children looked at each other, then the boy's chin
trembled and he began to cry. Barbara didn't know what to do.*

*'You don't have to eat that,' she told him. 'What do you like?
You can have whatever you like.'*

*The boy went on crying, but his sister piped up: 'He only likes
meat on the bone.'*

*Barbara was bewildered. 'You know,' the girl went on. 'Chops
that he can pick up and eat in his fingers. And I just like chips.'*

*Barbara was dismayed to have got off to a bad start with
the children and blamed Simon for not finding out this simple fact
from his ex-wife before the visit.*

As a step-parent you can only encourage your partner to keep
abreast of his children's lives and allow you to participate as
much as possible. In the last scenario everyone felt bad: Barbara
because she wanted to get off to a good start with her stepchildren,
Simon because he didn't know his children well enough, and
the children because everything was strange and they were being
asked to eat things they were not used to. It could all have been
different if Simon had made one five-minute phone-call.

'Should I love my stepchild?'

One of the biggest pressures the part-time step-parent faces (and
the full-time step-parent for that matter) is the pressure to 'love'
their stepchild. This pressure doesn't come from the child, far from

it, the child knows that he does not feel for the part-time step-parent the same way he does for his parents – why should he? No, this pressure comes from the parent. Understandably, when a parent loves their child they want their partner to love them in the same way, but parental love is a very specific emotion and cannot be replicated. This should not be a problem, because the sort of love a step-parent can eventually feel for his stepchild and vice versa is a good and solid alternative gradually built up over time, but it will always be different from the love a parent feels for his child, and is rarely achieved on a part-time acquaintance. Pressure on the part-time step-parent to love her stepchild and vice versa is doomed to breed resentment. She must give herself and her stepchild the space to get to know each other in their own time and and their own way and accept that part-time contact may never result in a very close relationship. Also she must avoid giving in to pressure from her partner to express a phoney emotion.

'Why can't I have more influence over my stepchild's life?'

This is a similar cry to the part-time parent but for different reasons. Many step-parents feel they have a more objective take on their stepchildren and can be helpful because of that, but do not feel in a position to speak their mind.

Emily was not an academic child, but both her parents had university degrees and were determined to channel her through college. Christine, her stepmother, saw Emily's talents more clearly and knew this insistence was a waste of time from everyone's point of view. She tried to talk to her partner, but her partner told her she didn't know Emily well enough and that Emily needed a degree and must be encouraged to make the effort. It drove Christine mad:

> I could see Emily was miserable and half-hearted at the prospect, and what worried me was that she would

deliberately fail her A levels so she wouldn't have to go to
college, or that she would flunk the first year of college for
the same reasons. I know it was subversive, but in the end
I talked to Emily myself. We weren't particularly close,
but she immediately appreciated having an ally . . . what
she wanted to do was to get into management and was
prepared to work her way up through the secretarial
route, which was what I had done and been very successful
doing it. I told her she would need good A levels for that
and that she must work hard but that I would do my
best to intercede on her behalf. I did manage to get my
husband to listen to his daughter in the end, but it was a
huge struggle. If I had not been so bossy I would have just
had to sit by and watch, which I expect is the fate of lots
of weekend stepmums. Emily didn't go to college in the
end and is currently earning almost as much as her father
in a high-powered management job!

A step-parent, whether weekend or full-time, has a right at least
to an opinion about her stepchild's welfare. If a part-time step-
parent takes an interest in her stepchild's life from the beginning
and isn't shy about speaking her mind to her partner, then
she stands a good chance of being included in discussions about
her stepchild's future. Most parents will welcome input from
their partner on the difficult problems of bringing up a child
successfully.

'How do I react when they endlessly compare me with their mother?'

Dogberry, in Shakespeare's *Much Ado About Nothing*, claims that
'Comparisons are odorous', and I think many step-parents would
agree. It is not necessarily malicious when a child says: 'Mum
makes her macaroni cheese with tomatoes,' and it is better not to
react as if it were. A child's world, particularly a young child's,

is very small and witnessing a different lifestyle at close quarters will inevitably bring comparisons, but these comparisons are often as much in the nature of observations as criticisms. Sometimes, if the step-relationship is hostile, the child will deliberately be trying to discomfort and criticize the step-parent, but the same rule applies: acknowledge the child, but don't over-react.

Jonty remembers deeply resenting his stepmother, whom he visited twice a month. Despite his stepmother being a very accomplished cook, or perhaps because of it, he would always complain about the food she cooked for him; he knew it was important to her and that she took a pride in her talent. But try as he might, he couldn't get her to rise to his taunts. His father would tell him off, but his stepmother was never anything but gracious. She would say: 'How interesting, Jonty, I've never tried mixing mustard with my mash, maybe I'll do it next time you come.' Or 'I'm sorry you don't like butter on your vegetables, I'll leave it off next time.' Or 'You must get your mother's recipe from her so I can try sausages her way.'

In the end he gave up and it became a joke between them. Years afterwards she admitted that she had wanted to kill him but refused to give him the satisfaction of knowing he was winding her up.

Easing the way for the full-time parent

The full-time parent has to let her child go to the weekend visits with his stepfamily with an enthusiastic attitude and not set up unnecessary conflict or competition between the two families. She also has to allow her child time to readjust after the visit. None of this is easy if the separation has been bitter and she is faced with the prospect of her child being under the care of a man she is perhaps hostile towards and a woman she might see as instrumental to her unhappiness. It is tempting for a parent to create animosity between her child and both her ex-partner and her ex-partner's lover, or to issue vindictive edicts about the presence of the lover, or decree punishing visiting times which are truncated, inflexible or in some way inconvenient to her ex-partner. It is tempting for her to cause a fuss about festivities, birthdays or holidays and complain about presents or treats given to the child. It is tempting for a resident parent to grill her child on his return and then criticize the other family to him.

All this is tempting, but none of it is advisable. No one will benefit, least of all the child, from giving in to the understandable desire to wreak revenge on those she sees as the cause of her pain. A step-parent can try to understand the full-time parent's position and avoid reacting with antagonistic behaviour which will again cause pain to her stepchild. The resident parent's position is further discussed in Chapter 6.

Reading this chapter you could be forgiven for thinking that part-time step-parenting is packed with problems. It is true there are potential problems, and obviously this book is for people experiencing those problems or wanting to know how to avoid them, but it is important to point out that it can also be fun once the initial wrinkles have been ironed out. So please don't despair.

To summarize:

* It is essential that a good dialogue be kept open between adults involved in the child's upbringing, be it full- or part-time. This is a top priority.

* Fighting between the adults involved, in front of the children, is unacceptable at any time.

* Keep in regular contact with your child, even if it's just a short phone call.

* Flexibility about visiting makes contact easier and less stressful for everyone.

* Children don't require endless *fun* on visits to their other family.

* A child must have space of his own in his part-time home.

* Parent and step-parent must co-operate in joint parenting of the children involved in the stepfamily.

* Special occasions must be shared fairly with the other family.

* Guilt is a wasteful and destructive emotion.

* Everyone needs time to get used to the part-time stepfamily situation.

And remember, enjoy yourself!

CHAPTER 5

The full-time stepfamily

Although statistics tell us that there are around seven times as many resident stepfathers today as there are resident stepmothers, and some research shows that these stepfathers are responsible for perpetrating a horrifying level of violence on their stepchildren, I believe strongly that the responsibility for the step-relationship rests squarely with both resident adults.

Before embarking upon the enormous responsibility of creating a full-time stepfamily, it is important for the adults concerned to take time to consider whether this is the best thing for themselves and the children involved. Two people may love each other deeply, but this doesn't necessarily mean they are either ready, or willing, to make the commitment that is essential for a successful step-family. Both parties must ask themselves some searching questions.

The step-parent's questions

Is this a long-term relationship?

Falling in love temporarily distorts a person's rational powers! Everything seems possible, including taking on a child or children whom they hardly know and may not even like. It is dangerous to rush into anything permanent in the early stages of a relationship where children are involved. They have been through the loss of one of their parents and don't need to lose another adult they have become close to. Obviously there are never any guarantees where relationships are concerned, but a lot of hurt can be avoided if the adults involved wait before making any permanent, residential commitments. Good relationships do not necessarily need to be conducted under the same roof!

'Do I like the child?'

This is key. Adults feel guilty about not liking children; they assume a child is a blank sheet, absent of all the adult characteristics responsible for engendering irritation and dislike. This is not so; children's personalities form very early. Also a child from a recently separated family is not at his best; he is perhaps having to deal with loss, anger, misplaced guilt and insecurity, all or any of which may make him hostile and difficult to get to know.

Before making any decisions it is best for the possible step-parent to give the child time to be seen at his best and to get to know him on a casual, pressure-free basis where neither adult nor child is threatened by commitment. If the step-parent can't get on with him on this type of acquaintance, then a residential arrangement at this stage might be disastrous. However, there is no need to despair. This does not mean the relationship with the child's parent is doomed; circumstances change, people get used to each other, children grow up and their priorities change. There is time.

'Am I ready to parent this child?'

Liking a child when the adult concerned has no responsibility for him, and actually parenting a child full-time, are not the same thing. The potential step-parent must ask himself if he is ready to be a parent, if he is prepared to make the endless sacrifices a parent has to make, for instance spending his money on the child and not on himself, forgoing a social event because there is no suitable baby-sitter, being woken in the night because the child is ill or unhappy, giving up his normal weekends to entertain him. These are things a parent does willingly because he loves his child and has a vested interest in his future, but a step-parent does it initially because he wants a permanent relationship with the child's parent. This is a good reason, but not such a compelling one, and as a result he will have to be consciously unselfish where a parent might be instinctively so.

A child looks to the resident parent of the same sex for an identification model. Someone taking on this role of resident step-parent must accept that the child will look to him for his model and be prepared for that responsibility.

The parent's questions

'Does he treat my child well?'

A parent is responsible for the welfare of her child. Even if she chooses to bring in another adult to share the responsibility of parenting, it is she and her child's other parent who are ultimately liable both emotionally, physically and legally for the safety and well-being of their child. Step-parents can, under some circum-stances, be given limited parental rights, but the buck finally stops with the birth-parent. As a child depends on his parents to protect him, it is essential for those parents to try to be objective about the way a new partner responds to their child before they decide on any long-term residential commitment.

When someone has been struggling as a lone parent following a separation, the thought of being a family once more and having another adult around with whom to share the daily happinesses and tribulations of family life can seem very attractive. This long-ing for stability can cloud a parent's judgement. She may over-look the fact that her new partner gets unnecessarily angry with the child over minor transgressions. She may overlook the fact that he often bullies her into leaving the child with someone unsuitable for the sake of a night out. She may overlook the fact that he never pays any attention to the child or seems irritated by the child's company. Deep in denial about her new partner's parental shortcomings, she murmurs to herself: 'It'll be fine once we're all living together.'

She is wrong … *it won't.*

A man who has been abusive in a previous relationship is likely to be abusive in any subsequent ones. Equally a man does not suddenly become an abuser by becoming a stepfather.

It is best for the parent to give them both time to rub the edges off, then try to make as realistic an assessment as possible. If she is even remotely worried about her partner's commitment to her child, then she should not bring him into the family yet.

'Does my child like him?'

Depending on how a parent introduces her new partner to her child, how long it is since the parental split and how old the child is at the time, there is a strong possibility that most children will take a while to get used to anyone brought into the family as a potential step-parent. The child may feel jealous, resentful of her parent's divided attention, or feel that her parent's new partner is somehow responsible for her grief. Taking these factors into account and, as always, giving everyone time to get to know each other, the parent will have to assess how much the child's hostility is really to do with the new partner and how much is as a result of her own agenda.

If a child has a very bad reaction to a parent's new partner then this is clearly not yet the time to introduce him into the family. Either she is not ready, there is a real personality clash between them, or he is treating her badly when the parent is not present. Talking to the child and giving her a chance to explain why she dislikes him should show up the real reason. It is very common for a parent to dismiss a child's genuine grievance as childish jealousy or bolshiness.

'Can I trust my partner with my child?'

This question is as important as regards a stepmother as a step-father. Statistics appear to suggest that the physical and sexual violence perpetrated on children is more the responsibility of the stepfather, but stepmothers are also capable of sadistic and mani-pulative behaviour with their stepchildren, often in a much more subtle way which leaves no outward scars. It is not helpful to identify men as the sole perpetrators of crimes against children. It also must not be forgotten that once a new partner takes up residence with the family, she will have the same access to the child as the parent does.

Cruelty to children, unfortunately, goes on in every type of family, not just stepfamilies, but stepchildren are particularly vul-nerable and a parent introducing a stranger into the home must be as sure as possible that they have the child's best interests at heart. (This is discussed in detail later in the chapter.)

If, after time and consideration, the adults concerned can answer all the above questions in the affirmative, then it is time to get together and discuss how they would both parent the child in the event of being co-parents. Things like financial commitment, disciplinary and lifestyle philosophy, whether they both want more children and how much the step-parent will be involved in decision-making for the child's future must all be debated. It isn't going to work if one adult favours corporal punishment, bed at six, large families, strict table manners and single-sex schooling, while the other shudders at the thought of more children and prefers a liberal regime in both domestic and educational terms. People may think they wouldn't fall in love with someone with such opposing views, but they would be wrong, it happens all the time, and the differences are only exposed when disagreements surface with regard to parenting the children. Compromises are inevitable, but the co-parents must agree on a basic parenting philosophy to have any chance of making their stepfamily work. Here are some of the things they should consider:

* How much will the step-parent be involved in decisions about his stepchild?

* Who will be financially responsible for the child? If it is the absent parent, is the arrangement satisfactory?

* Do both adults want more children in the relationship? Often the partner who has children already is not keen to start another family.

* Do both adults agree about corporal punishment? Hitting a child is never advisable, but they must agree.

* Are discipline and manners important to both the co-parents? If they are, then bratty children who stay up till midnight causing mayhem are not the best foundation for a relationship, especially if they aren't yours.

* Do both sides agree on education? Many couples fall out over this. Do they have the same goals for the child?

* Do they agree about who should be responsible for child care? Even these days there are men who object to their wives working, or refuse to take any part in child care.

Agreement on these issues is fundamental to family harmony; both parent and step-parent may have to compromise in some areas, but opening the discussion provides a basis to refer back to if things go wrong.

All things considered, the adults concerned decide to make a long-term commitment and become a stepfamily. There's no reason to assume that things won't go well if they have gone into the commitment with care, but let's identify some of the problems they might face in the early stages.

What is the new stepchild feeling?

'I'm angry ...'

Children joining stepfamilies today are, on average, under ten years old. This probably means that the child has had little or no choice in the matter and this powerlessness can create immediate resentment. Also, the fact of a new partner for his parent will destroy any dream he might be nursing that his parents can be reunited – a mother remarrying will even have a different surname to himself. He may be very angry with his parent for bringing another adult into his home, but he won't necessarily direct the anger towards the parent. When a child has been through a family break-up he will feel insecure about his parents, and to be angry with the one he lives with and depends upon might seem too dangerous, so he will subconsciously divert his anger towards the intruder, in this case the unsuspecting step-parent.

This can be very hard to deal with for a well-meaning step-parent who is bending over backwards to accommodate a new stepchild. He can't change the way the child feels about his intrusion, but if he understands that the anger is not really personal to him, but an expression of overall anger at the situation the child finds himself in, then it will be easier to tolerate and he will probably find it is short-lived. The step-parent should try to talk to his stepchild, explain that he understands how difficult the change in his domestic arrangements must be for him and ask him if there is anything he can do to make it easier. The fact that he has acknowledged the child's distress will probably be enough to open the lines of communication between step-parent and stepchild that will be so vital in the months to come.

Nina remembers being 'a pig' to her stepfather, Colin, when he first moved in with her mother. She was ten at the time and she says:

> I followed him around and every time he did something I
> told him we didn't do it like that or that Mummy wouldn't

like it that way. Stupid things like the way he tied up the bin-bags. I said he had to tie them with string and not just knot them at the top because Mummy said they weren't so secure just knotted. He was amazing, he went along with it all though he must have known it wasn't true because he talked to Mum. That's one thing children forget, that adults tell each other everything. One Sunday morning he was up early cooking breakfast . . . he was really kind to us all and it makes me sad to think how horrible I was to him . . . anyway, he had cooked these pancakes with maple syrup and bacon. I loved them, but there was no way I was going to let him know. Mum wasn't up yet, but he made me a big plate of breakfast and set it down in front of me. I remember the feeling so well, it was a horrible twisted feeling which was a combination of being angry and not wanting to be angry . . . I think I was sort of trapped in my anger. I could see how hard he was trying to be nice and that made me even more irritated. Anyway, there was this scrummy plate of food which smelled divine and a little jug of syrup just waiting to be gobbled, and I refused to eat it, I couldn't eat it, but I so wanted to. Mad . . . I just looked at his eager face and said sulkily: 'I don't like pancakes and bacon,' and pushed the plate away. Colin never missed a beat. He picked up the plate quite calmly and threw the lot in the bin. 'Never mind,' he said. 'You can make yourself some toast instead.' He had called my bluff.

I thought I might get into trouble from Mum when she came down, because she knew I adored pancakes and bacon, but he never told on me, and if he did then Mum very sensibly refused to react. I think that breakfast was some sort of a turning point in my relationship with Colin. I felt so beastly behaving the way I did, and his own behaviour was exemplary. The next time pancakes were on the menu I said very quickly that I'd changed my mind and I liked them now!

'You're not my father ...'

This is true. A step-parent should not pretend to be, not try to be, and not even suggest that he is. He should let the child understand up front that he knows she has two parents, wherever they may be, and that he is very much a step-parent. It is a good idea for him to explain that he wants to care for his stepchild, but that he doesn't intend to, and never will, replace her absent parent. In time he may in fact do so, especially if his stepchild is young when he takes up residence, but that is for the future. He can talk about what she would like to call him, but avoid 'Dad' or 'Mum'. There are situations where a child calls her step-parent 'Dad' or 'Mum', usually when the absent parent has lost touch with the child at a very early age, but it is important to keep the distinction clear in a child's mind, otherwise she may have trouble later with who she really is, perhaps believing her stepfather is her real father.

'She'll change everything ...'

Reasonably enough, one of the child's main fears when a step-parent hoves over the horizon is that everything will change. Already the child will have had to go through one life-altering experience, perhaps moving house, moving school, losing touch with extended-family members, and possibly adjusting to a different regime at home with only one parent's disciplinary philosophy to take into account. The advent of a step-parent threatens his security yet again. Maybe he won't be allowed to stay up late on a Saturday, maybe he won't be able to help his mother with the weekly shop, maybe he won't be able to share his mother's bed, maybe there's talk of moving again, or redecoration, or a change of a beloved holiday venue, different food, different friends, different rules ...

Of course a new person entering a family will bring new ideas and different ways of doing things, it is right that they should, and with time the child will probably appreciate this, but changing too much too quickly will only increase her sense of insecurity. The adults in the stepfamily should make any changes slowly and try to involve the child as much as possible. For instance, if the family needs to move for space reasons they can explain this to the child and consult her about the choice of the new house and the decorations, especially her own bedroom.

It is also best not to alter her living patterns all at once. If she has always stayed up and watched *Casualty* with her mum, then she should still be allowed to. If she has always slept in her mother's bed, then she should be weaned off the habit slowly before the new step-parent moves in, perhaps with the offer of something new as an incentive, like a duvet cover or bedside lamp. If she isn't used to babysitters then it would be best to start with a trusted aunt or grandmother rather than the teenager from down the road.

Beverly's stepfather was extremely rich. Before the remarriage Beverly and her mum had had to struggle with money, always having to think before they bought anything, worrying about the rent and seldom having any treats. Beverly remembers liking her future stepfather at first, but within days of her mother announcing that they would marry, they had packed the small flat up, throwing most of their 'junk' away, and were swept off to her stepfather's large and luxurious mansion. Beverley's mum thought her daughter would be thrilled to escape from all the worry and be able to have what she wanted, and when Beverly sulked she was furious with her and told her she was selfish and spoilt, that she didn't know how unhappy she had been without a husband etc. etc. . . . but Beverly felt bereft of everything that was familiar to her and felt she had no place in her stepfather's world.

> Me and mum were poor, yes, but we were cosy enough and I thought we'd been happy. It was a shock to know that Mum had been so miserable with me. Also Mum was ashamed of our furniture and things and insisted we threw them out, so I wasn't even allowed to take my bunk bed, which I loved and had painted all over with sea horses and

stuff. I was taken shopping for new clothes and you'd think
a girl of nine would love that, but all the old sweaters
and jeans had to go too because Mum didn't think they
would 'fit in'. He wasn't the king or anything. When we
moved in she went on and on about my table manners and
sitting with my legs crossed and stupid stuff like that.
I absolutely loathed him. Not Mum . . . him. He couldn't
do right and if he'd died I would have danced on his grave.
I really felt my childhood had been ruined. I admit I behaved
badly, but it was all so sudden and I felt bewildered and
lost . . . betrayed. I still get wound up thinking about it,
even fifteen years on.

'I feel left out . . . '

There is a saying, 'The children of lovers are orphans'; and how
hard it is to think of anyone else when you are in love. But if
a parent suddenly withdraws too much attention from her child
he will certainly resent the new recipient of her favours. This
is particularly true of the same-sex child. A son may feel he has
become the man of the family since the separation and takes
a pride in protecting his mother; a daughter may feel she has been
important in caring for her father and feel very bitter when he
suddenly does not appear to need her any more.

*Diane had been divorced from her husband for five years when
she met William:*

We just fell madly in love. It was so great to feel that way
again, there had been times when I thought I never would.
Dan was nine at the time and I suppose we had been
quite a duo since Martin left. I just didn't realize quite how
much I was leaving him out until he did something terrible.
We had a lodger who was at London University studying
law. Her finals were coming up and she was working every
hour God sent, but she was a sweet girl and got on really

well with Danny. One day when she was at college, Dan went into her room, which was on the top floor next to his, and destroyed four files full of essays and revision notes. He just tore each carefully written page into small pieces and left them on the bed. Sheena was devastated of course, as was I. Dan denied it at first, but eventually he broke down and told me how awful life was with William around and how I never paid him any attention, etc. . . . he cited two nights when he'd waited till after midnight for me to come and say goodnight as I'd promised, that the previous week he'd had babysitters four nights in a row, that William opened the wine bottles now and that he felt I didn't need him any more. I'd been so wrapped up in the affair that I literally hadn't given poor Dan a thought. I was so ashamed because I felt I'd let him down and also that I was the one really responsible for Sheena's notes. Luckily she got a first anyway. William and I were more careful after that, but it's extremely difficult being a parent in love.

A parent with a new partner is advised not to change too much too quickly for her child. It is better for the parent to try to continue the normal routine as much as possible and to give her child plenty of time without the presence of her new partner.

'They make me feel guilty . . .'

Back to the impossible question of how to control the jealousies and irritations with an ex-partner. The answer is that most people probably can't, but what they can do is avoid involving their child. It is fine for a separated parent to rant and rage as much as he likes to his friends, to (or at) his 'ex', to his new partner, to himself, but he should do it away from the eyes and ears of his offspring. It just isn't fair for him to burden them with his unresolved pain and bitterness. It isn't fair to make them feel bad when they have had a great day with their other parent, it isn't fair to prejudice them against their step-parent so that they have to pretend not to like them. It isn't fair to question them about the other family's lifestyle just so that the jealous adult can carp and criticize and so undermine the child's confidence. The parent concerned must find a way, whatever it is, to keep their feelings to themselves.

'I'm caught in the middle ...'

Children can get very confusing messages when parents have diverse ideologies, especially if this diversity is used as a competitive parenting tool. What does a parent do when his son comes home with a toy pistol his mother has presented him with when he has always forbidden the children to play with replica weapons and he knows his wife knows it? What does a parent do when her daughter comes home with a video game from her father when she considers them time-consuming and detrimental to her child's school work and social skills? To confiscate the present will only build resentment and open the door for more confrontation of the same ilk. This week a pistol, next week a Kalashnikov.

All a parent can do is explain to his child that his views on guns or video games have not changed and remind him what they are and the reason for them. The child may not agree with his parent, but he should respect his position. His parent can then tell him that if he wants guns he must keep them at his mother's house. Parents, whether together or separated, are entitled to differing opinions, but it is unhelpful to the child if, by undermining each other's views to score points, he is left uncomfortably in the middle. It is important for parents to sort out a position before their child reaches the age where he has much more important conflicts to deal with – their parental position on smoking, drugs and violence, for instance.

What are the responsibilities and dilemmas of the adults in the stepfamily?

Protect the child

Making a child completely safe is, unfortunately, an impossible task. However careful the adults in a family are, unpredictable things happen and people in a position of trust sometimes betray that trust. Aside from the unpredictable, though, there are some simple rules that the adults in a stepfamily can employ to minimize the risk to their child. This is true for any family, not just a stepfamily.

* An adult suffering from substance addiction such as drugs or alcohol poses a threat to those around him, particularly to a child. Any person aware of such a situation should take action to protect the child. The action taken will depend on the severity of the problem, but start by talking to the person concerned. If this has no effect, then it will be necessary to take it further, to a doctor, or ultimately the social services or police.

* An adult prone to using violence as a solution to a problem is a similar threat. Again, action must be taken.

* Clear sexual boundaries should be established within a stepfamily to protect both adult and child. Bathing and dressing should be done in private and the privacy of the individual should be respected by everyone.

* Children must know they will be listened to and treated with respect if they complain of any sort of abuse or manipulative behaviour from an adult or sibling either inside or outside the stepfamily. (This is true for any family.)

* Adults should take seriously signs of distress in a child such as unaccustomed bedwetting, soiling, sleeping problems, eating problems or withdrawn or disruptive behaviour. If these signs are present it is vital to talk to the child or seek outside help by visiting a doctor.

* If a full-time stepfather or stepmother finds it hard to treat a stepchild with proper kindness and care, they should move out of the family home, at least in the short term, rather than stay and risk violence or even minor cruelty to the child in question. Step-parenting is difficult at the best of times, but the adults in a relationship do not necessarily need to live under the same roof.

Maintaining an open and respectful relationship between all members of a stepfamily is the best protection against abuse of any kind within the family group.

The step-parent and the absent parent

A step-parent is in no position to criticize her stepchild's absent parent. Now this might be tempting, especially when she can see that contact with the parent upsets the child, but children are strangely loyal even to seriously defective parents. They may feel themselves to be in a position to complain that their mother is selfish and doesn't care, and their step-parent may know this to be true, but a stepchild won't thank the step-parent for agreeing and joining in the criticism. This position tends to change as the child grows up and has more clarity and less dependency on his parent, but until then the step-parent must walk a tightrope, supporting the stepchild as much as he will allow, but keeping out of the relationship with his parents as much as possible.

Elena was a full-time stepmother to Josh. His mother had married again but Josh had a difficult relationship with his stepfather so

*had been shipped out to live with his father when he was ten.
Josh visited his old home as little as possible, but stayed for at least
a week every school holiday. Whenever he returned from staying
with them he would be tense, insecure, moody and unhappy.
Elena got to the stage where she dreaded the visits as much
as Josh did:*

> It was a nightmare. I would spend the better part of two
> weeks getting him back on track. Josh said that through-
> out every visit his mother would undermine him, criticize
> him and jibe at me and his father and our way of life. I was
> very angry with them both, but Josh entirely blamed his
> stepfather, I suppose it was easier than accepting that
> his mother had let him down. I had to bite my tongue and
> just listen to his unhappiness. I suggested he stop visiting,
> but understandably he couldn't let go. I think he kept
> hoping that she would change, or at least apologize.
>
> One day, after a particularly stupid and mean letter that
> had really upset Josh, I just lost my temper and started
> ranting about how weak and selfish she was and how
> cruel she had been to him and how he deserved better.
> I was fully supporting what he knew to be true, but
> he couldn't cope with my saying so and was very angry
> with me and even more upset. I felt bad for the out-
> burst, but years later Josh told me that actually it had
> comforted him.

Depending on the relationship with a partner's 'ex', in the early
stages it is probably better for a step-parent to stay in the back-
ground as far as dealings with the other parent are concerned.
It is best for them to let their partner make visiting arrangements
and attend school functions alone. In time it may be possible for
the step-parent to be included, or to agree to separate attendances
at their stepchild's school play, concert or sporting event. She
can discuss with her stepchild what he wants her to do, and let
him know she is interested and keen to be involved in these events

if he feels comfortable with it. He does not want his stepmother and his other parent spitting venom at each other across the school football pitch. One stepchild said she would definitely elope when the time came for her to marry because she couldn't bear the thought of her parents and steps all sitting in an angry row in the front of the church not speaking to each other. It's better for the child if everyone can get on, but if the step-parent isn't given the chance then it is best for her to take a back seat until the situation improves.

It is also vital not to get involved in competitive parenting. A child will inevitably make comparisons between a parent and step-parent of the same sex, but even when she voices these comparisons as a criticism of her step-parent's methods, skills or philosophies, it does not help for the step-parent to take offence; she should stick to her guns and explain gently to her stepchild that her ways are neither better nor worse but merely different to those of her parent.

Tom was under a constant barrage of criticism from his two teen-aged stepsons, aged fourteen and sixteen when he first married their mother. Apparently Tom was untidy whereas their father was immaculate. Tom's car was old whereas their father's was brand-spanking new. Tom was useless with his hands whereas their father could build or fix anything. Tom had a bit of a paunch but their father was slim and fit. Tom's job was less prestigious than their father's, etc, etc.

They were both very subtle about the way they criticized, but it never stopped and I think it became a habit which was fed by their father whenever they visited him for a weekend. I never thought of myself as particularly competitive and I always ignored their taunts, but I real-ized the carping was making me dread my stepchildren's company. It wasn't as if I had been in any way responsible for the break-up of their family, I had come on the scene

years after their father had run off with another woman.
I suppose they resented my presence but also I think
they were trying to persuade themselves that he was an
OK person when they knew really he was thoroughly
selfish and mean.

In the end I decided to confront them. I chose an
evening when my wife was out at her art class, then
bought some Cokes and snacks and sat them down in the
sitting-room. They both looked nervous and defensive
before I had even opened my mouth so I knew it wouldn't
be easy. I handed them a piece of paper each and a biro
and said: 'I want you to write down all the things about
me that you don't like. You obviously have a lot of criticisms and I think the best thing is to air them, discuss them
and then we don't need to mention them again.'

They looked gob-smacked and the eldest threw down
the paper and said he wouldn't do it. I asked him why not
and he wouldn't answer. Anyway, as a ploy it worked
because they knew they couldn't intimidate me any more.
I explained that we might as well get on if we were to live
together, but that it wasn't for ever and I told them that
they must love their father very much and that he was
lucky to have such loyalty from his children. They looked
very sheepish and didn't say much at the time, but having
it out in the open meant if they did it again I could joke
about it and it made me feel much better. Of course, once
they knew I'd got their number they stopped winding
me up and we got along much better.

I think I felt that as a stepfather I didn't have any rights
or authority, that I was somehow in an inferior position
to their father, and I think a lot of step-parents feel
like that.

Resident parent as pig-in-the-middle

The step-parent must understand that although the parent in the stepfamily is the link between him and her child, this position is open to abuse because the 'link' is often a woman and women tend to be the peacemakers in most families. She can find herself constantly acting as a go-between between step-parent and step-child. Not only will this position be very stressful, but it will also prevent the step-parent and stepchild ever forging a relationship together. This is discussed at greater length in the following chapter.

His, hers and ours

When two adults get together who both have children from a previous relationship in residence, then decide to have a child of their own, there is a wealth of different relationships within one family. One of the advantages of this combination is that there are two sets of children in the same situation, i.e. they are step-siblings to each other and have a step- and a birth-parent in residence. Also the adults are both parents and step-parents, so understand the emotions involved in these commitments. The problem these stepfamilies have over and above the less varied stepfamily is the practical one of the family being large, and the fact that the access visits with the absent parents are complicated and time-consuming, the result being that the family spends more leisure time apart than together and has little opportunity to blend the various groups.

Sylvia remembers her home being in a constant state of chaos. There were six children, three her stepfather's, two her mother's and one half-sibling. Each weekend would be a battle about who would take whom where, when everyone needed picking up, how the homework and social life would be fitted in.

> It was like the scene of a disaster by Sunday night . . . over-
> night bags from visits to our other parents full of dirty
> clothes, homework not done, everyone wanting to talk
> about their weekend, some of us needing food, others not,
> everyone tired, our half-sibling screaming to play with us
> because he'd been deserted all weekend. I honestly
> don't know how our parents coped.

There are no easy solutions on offer to this one, but it helps if
the household is as organized as possible and the absent partners
appreciate the situation and help out wherever possible. Look
on the bright side, family life will never be dull!

Financial support

Because money is never simply about money, but about emotions
as well, this is a very complex subject which affects everyone in
the separated family and the stepfamily. It is discussed in
Chapter 8.

The birth of half-siblings

The birth of a half-sibling can be a great way to bring a stepfamily
together, because the new baby is related to all the family members
and gives them a common cause. However, it can also be the
focus of jealousy, guilt and resentment. For a step-parent it can be
hard to reconcile the intense feeling of being a parent with the
more detached and possibly contentious relationship he has with
his stepchild. He might feel guilty for feeling differently about
his new baby. A parent who had hoped the baby would unite the
family might be angry if their older child does not appear to be
playing the game.

Any new baby can create jealousy in its siblings, but this is particularly true of half-siblings. The new baby is the birth-child of both adults in the stepfamily; he belongs in a way the stepchild never can. Unless the adults are very careful, the stepchild will be only too aware of the difference and resent the baby for having the parental love and security that he feels he has lost. The baby's birth will also underline the cementing of the new relationship, something the stepchild might find difficult to accept if he is still coming to terms with his parents' divorce.

A parent will love her first-born as much as any subsequent children, but she will be able to share the new baby with her partner in a way she may not have been able to share her child from her first marriage, and this closeness is all too easily communicated to her older children.

A step-parent can avoid these pitfalls by remembering the following:

> * It is best not to rush into having another child too early in a new relationship. A new stepchild and his step-parent need to establish their relationship before the advent of another child. Many parents worry about the gap between their first family and any subsequent children, but another year won't make any significant difference to anyone.

> * The adults in the stepfamily need to prepare the existing child very carefully for the birth of her half-sibling. Many parents in this position fail to tell their children till late on in the pregnancy because they are worried about their reaction. Include the child in all the preparations and ensure that friends and relatives, especially the step-parent's family, include her too.

> * The differences between this birth and the previous one need not be emphasized to the existing child. It is easy for a parent in the optimism of a new relationship to say things such as: 'I'm so happy you want to be there for

the birth . . . so-and-so couldn't bear the thought.' 'It's going to be so much better with you as the father . . . so-and-so was never home.' 'I'll be a much better mother this time with you to support me.' Saying these things in front of the child will only make her feel second best.

∗ All the children in the stepfamily should be treated in the same way. This is very important. It can be tempting for a step-parent to lavish attention, money and space on his own child at the expense of his stepchild. Don't boot the stepchild out of her bedroom to make room for the baby. Don't give numerous presents to the baby but not to the older child. Don't use the older stepchild as a convenient babysitter.

∗ The adults in the stepfamily should not expect the existing child to be as thrilled as they are about the birth of a half-sibling. It might take the child some time to adjust to the idea and she shouldn't be pressured into phoney enthusiasm.

With a bit of thought and planning the birth of a half-sibling can offer security and companionship to the stepchild and give her a real sense of belonging.

To adopt or not to adopt?

Adoption is a big step. Many step-parents think it best for themselves, their partner and their stepchild to legalize their position of full-time responsibility for their stepchild. (By the way, you are only legally a step-parent if you are married to your partner.) The step is usually taken when the child has lost touch with his other parent for some reason, and gives shared and equal responsibility to the adults in the stepfamily for the caring and upbringing of the children by a previous partner. The child can take the stepfather's surname if he wishes and along with the step-parent's own children will be entitled to an equal share of the step-parent's estate when he dies. However, all maintenance and inheritance rights from the other parent and his family will be lost, and all contact rights will be terminated.

It is a very serious decision to cut all links between a child and his parent. The child may feel confused later as to who he really is and resent the parent concerned for taking away his family name and breaking ties with his other parent. It may be clear to everyone that the absent parent is not fit to be a parent for some reason, but that parent and his relatives will always be the child's blood family.

Some reasons to consider adoption

Unfit parent

If the child's absent parent is someone generally considered unfit to parent their child, then adoption offers more security in the event of important decisions needing to be made about the child's future, especially in the event of the resident parent dying, because the adoptive parent will remain responsible for the child in these circumstances and the child's absent parent will not have the legal right to take charge of the child.

Inheritance

Adoption is perhaps the simplest way to ensure that a stepchild receives an equal share of a step-parent's inheritance. However, a carefully considered will can have the same effect.

Sharing the family name

Many stepfamilies consider it simpler to have all the family bearing the same name for practical reasons and reasons of family unity.

Commitment

Some step-parents feel very strongly that they want this ultimate legal commitment to a child they love.

Some reasons *not* to consider adoption

Cementing the family

It is common for the adults in a stepfamily to try to resolve conflicts by considering adoption, on the premise that 'If we're a proper family things will be easier.' If the family is not working as it is, then it is unlikely that adoption will improve the situation.

Punishing the absent parent

Unfortunately parents often use adoption as a tool with which to punish the deserting parent by legally depriving him of access to his children. As always, it is the child who suffers most.

Step-parent as mediator

All is not gloom and doom. Many step-parents feel that because they are not as emotionally involved with their stepchild as their partner is, they can offer some perspective when things go wrong between parent and child.

Stephen has two stepdaughters, but the eldest, Frances, has a very tempestuous relationship with her mother, he thinks because they are so alike.

Many a day when Frances was younger they would have a real set-to about something and Frances would stamp off and fling herself on her bed to sob her heart out. Jill was always too angry and proud to make the first move, and so there'd be stalemate for days if I didn't do something about it. Because I wasn't exactly related, Frances could see me as an ally, someone almost like a mate. She would rant on about her mother and I could sympathize without the complication of the parental bond. It is good to have a relationship like that to alleviate that family closeness that can become suffocating at times.

A viable alternative

Most parents fall into the role of parenting without too much thought. They tend to parent in the way their parents have parented them, perhaps with only the modifications a different generation imposes. This may be fine for the child, it may not be, but in most cases it won't be particularly considered, so the same mistakes can be perpetrated down the generations: 'My mum always … and I survived.'

A step-parent has the chance to focus on his parenting role. This means that parenting will keep him on his toes, he will have to make the effort a birth-parent will not, be on the look-out for problems and be sensitive to interactions that a birth-parent will take for granted, but the end result could be that he becomes a better parent.

Jim has just seen his youngest stepchild off to university.

It ain't over yet, and I won't say it hasn't been a real stress at times … you have to keep your wits about you because it's not a natural process like having your own kids. But I'll say this. For me it's been a viable alternative, a real family, and I reckon the ups and downs we've had are no more or less than the average family and because we're a 'step' we've taken a bit more care to get it right. Nothing wrong with that, eh?

To summarize:

Stepfamilies can work, and work well, when sensitively handled and given time. Here are some of the things to watch out for:

* ✱ Don't enter a full-time commitment lightly.

* ✱ Work out a joint parenting philosophy that you can both agree on.

* ✱ Don't change too much too fast in the child's life.

* ✱ Make clear to your stepchild that you are not trying to replace his absent parent.

* ✱ Treat the arrival of half-siblings with great care.

* ✱ Treat all children in the stepfamily exactly the same as regards love, discipline, time, space and material things.

* ✱ The child in the family should be treated with care and respect. This includes avoiding criticism of the absent parent in the child's presence.

* ✱ All adults responsible for a child's welfare should be able to communicate with each other without open hostility.

* ✱ Separate financial discussions from emotional ones (see Chapter 8).

* ✱ Remember that stepfamilies, like Rome, aren't built in a day.

CHAPTER 6

The role of the birth-parent in the stepfamily

Since most step-parents must, to some degree, deal with their partner's ex-partner, and also be sensitive to their partner's role as a parent, it is important for them to understand some of the fears and insecurities that being a separated parent involves, not least the enormous jealousy that can be engendered by the advent of a step-parent. By understanding, they can perhaps help to prevent some of the unnecessary turmoil these insecurities create. This chapter examines the position of both the resident parent and the part-time parent with children they must share.

The parents from a separated relationship have two possible roles. One is as the resident parent, the other is as the absent parent. Both have the possibility of bringing another adult into their lives and so creating a stepfamily. Both retain the responsibility for their child's welfare even in the presence of step-parents.

What is the single, resident parent facing?

It is hard enough for any adult to face the breakdown of their relationship, to accept that their family has to separate and that contact between children and parents is now something that has to be formalized, haggled over and restricted. It is just as hard for someone to accept that their ex-partner now has a new partner and is creating a new family for their child, albeit on a part-time basis, and that they will have to give their child over to that family for periods of time. How can they best cope with all this?

Punishing an ex-partner

When a parent has been deserted, the one weapon she has against her ex-partner is the children. This is a very powerful weapon. She can impose guilt, pain and vast inconvenience on him from her position as resident parent, controlling him with edicts about the step-parent or about visiting arrangements which, if disobeyed, will threaten his ability to see his children. She can also poison the children against the step-parent, so that they never enjoy an unbiased view of her.

Bonnie was devastated when Mike walked out on their marriage and their two children, then aged four and six, to take up with his secretary.

> It was a such a predictable scenario, such a cliché. I will never forget the pain and the disbelief; I genuinely had a problem believing he had gone, and that he wasn't coming back. I wanted so badly to hurt him, to let him feel the pain I was feeling, and whenever he came to take the children out I would give it to him . . . he would say something in-nocuous like 'How have the kids been?' and I would start: 'How do think they've been? Billy's had nightmares all week, Ellie's cried over stupid things. Neither of them understand what you've done, you're a bastard, a thought-less, cruel bastard, you have no idea how you've ruined their lives just to satisfy your pathetic testosterone urges with that trollop,' etc, etc. He was feeling hideous guilt, I knew him well enough to know that, so he would get defensive and we would shout and scream at each other until he would grab the kids and rush off and I would spend the next few hours crying and ranting against the injustice of it all.

If he'd only apologized, but he blamed me! Said I didn't understand him and that she did. It all seems so stupid now, but at the time I felt as if I was dying.

One day we were having our usual argument on the doorstep, and the children had joined us. We hardly noticed them, we were so busy cursing each other, but suddenly Ellie let out a terrible wail of grief. We both turned to them and realized they were both crying, Billy clutching his hands over his ears to block out our row, Ellie shouting 'Stop it, Mummy, stop it.' It was a real shock to us both. We stopped at once. Amazingly enough, neither of us had really taken in how upset the children would be to see us at each other's throats. We made a vow that from then on we would try not to argue in front of them, and we succeeded most of the time.

Another example:

Tom also ran off with his PA:

I never thought Ginny would be so vindictive . . . I knew she'd be difficult, but I was in denial about the kids, I just thought we'd work it out fine in the end . . . the reality was hell. She banned me from letting them meet Brenda, which I suppose was fair enough at first, but not fair two years down the line. She made every arrangement impossible for me, changing things at the last minute and using every excuse in the book to deny me my proper weekend visits: dentists, grandparents, kids' parties, so that my time got whittled down to almost nothing. Then she would say I could ring on Wednesday night, but when I rang she said the girls couldn't come to the phone. I wasn't allowed to buy them presents or do anything that might be fun and they'd be interrogated when they got back so they were always on edge with me. She must have poisoned them against me because they would say things like:

'Mummy says you have loads of money but you don't want to give us any . . . Mummy says your girlfriend is a bitch . . . '

I was in despair. I knew I had behaved badly, but to my mind she was behaving just as badly, if not worse, with her vicious manipulations. And no one was getting any benefit, not her, not me, not the children. Particularly not the children. We never resolved it . . . but the children eventually grew up.

These two sad, cautionary tales are enough to illustrate the need to control any impulse a separated parent may have to use the children as weapons against their ex-partner. As Tom said: 'No one was getting any benefit . . . particularly not the children.' There are some truths that may help in the quest for a workable relationship with an ex-partner:

* Manipulative and hysterical behaviour only enforces an ex-partner's justification for apportioning blame.

* Getting on with an ex-partner is probably a better revenge as far as a rival is concerned than fighting with him; it might make her insecure. (Revenge is childish but nonetheless comforting!)

* Children can like their step-parent without it affecting their relationship with their parent even remotely. There is no need to be competitive on this score.

* The more a person practises politeness the easier it gets.

* Seeing an ex-partner in their new context helps to make the truth of it more acceptable and easier to bear. Not seeing them can prolong the fantasy.

* Some days will be better than others. It is sensible to avoid the 'ex' on bad ones.

* The only ones who may not recover from the hostilities between warring parents are the children.

Leaning too heavily on the child

Separating from a partner, for someone not involved in another relationship, can be a lonely business. The adult can be tempted to lean very heavily on her children, particularly the eldest, sharing with them her grief and rage at the desertion. By treating them like another adult she is assuming they can understand and appreciate adult emotions such as sexual jealousy, manipulation and betrayal, and although children experience pain as intensely as adults, the nuances of adult relationships can be baffling and frightening to a child. It is also true that children find it hard to watch the adult they depend upon in a state of unceasing distress. It would be wrong for her not to show her grief at all, to bottle it up and pretend that everything is fine – a child whose world has been shattered would be just as baffled by this sort of behaviour – but allowing them to witness an uncontrolled display of emotion will be very frightening, however much they appear to understand and sympathize. They have just lost the reassuring presence of the other parent, and her distress might threaten their security still further if she appears to be unable to cope. It also will be detracting from any problems they might have, making them wary of telling their parent what is troubling them for fear of upsetting her further.

For a parent finding it hard to cope with the family splitting up, and there are few who would not, there are usually many places to seek help outside the immediate family. They can talk to a close friend, a sibling, or a counsellor. It is all right for a parent to let her child know she is unhappy, but she should as much as possible reserve her obvious distress for times when the children are not present. She should also give them the chance to cry, and cry with them, but try not to frighten them or be too cruel about her ex-partner, who is, after all, their other parent. Once something is said, even if it's spoken in the understandable extremes of anger and pain, it can be remembered by a child, and possibly taken out of context, long after the adult concerned has forgotten and moved on.

Rob will never forget the weeks and months following his father's defection with their young babysitter.

> Mum had always been so quiet before Dad left, not at all the neurotic type, although I suppose I never really thought about it at the time, I was only eleven. Dad managed it very badly. He told us on Christmas Eve . . . imagine. I still can't get my head round it. Would three more days have been so terrible? He says he just couldn't bear the thought of deceiving us all any more and pretending to be happy, so he just ran away.
>
> Anyway, as you can imagine, Mum was hysterical, it was as if someone had literally blown her up, she just ceased to function. I've got two younger sisters, and I had to be responsible and try to hide Mum's crying and stuff from them because I thought they would be frightened, but the truth was that I was frightened too. I genuinely thought she was so unhappy she would die, because she kept repeating 'I just want to die . . . I just want to die . . . there's no point in living . . .' etc. I took to following her from room to room to make sure she was OK and checking up on her at night so that in the end I wasn't sleeping properly at all. Dad was no use at all, he just didn't want to know, and we didn't have any family close by. It was utter hell. Mum even started smoking . . . she'd always been dead against smoking.
>
> Things calmed down in the end, but I never felt I could rely on either of my parents again.

Once a parent, always a parent

To a child a parent is always first and foremost a parent. As a child grows up they may also see their parents as friends, but they are still primarily their parents and they will look to them to fulfil the parental role to some degree even into adulthood. This does not change whether a parent is married, separated, divorced, widowed or remarried. Many people experiencing the breakdown of a relationship make a conscious effort to change themselves, thinking their personality or lifestyle has in some way been to blame for their partner's rejection. There is nothing wrong with this, in many cases the person is merely reverting to a more natural persona which has been smothered by the marriage, but however much a person may alter their way of life, the children must still be the first priority until they reach maturity.

Andrea's mother and father separated when she was in her teens. Her mother then seemed to lose all sense of responsibility for her daughter:

> She suddenly wanted to come with me to the pub and hang out with my friends. I know she was lonely and I felt sorry for her, but it was so embarrassing, especially when she began to dress as if she was in her twenties rather than her forties. She wouldn't let me call her Mum any more, I had to call her Susan . . . 'I'm not just your mother, you know,' she said, 'I have my own identity.' I knew that, but she *was* still my mother.

Dealing with the step-parent

It is one thing for an adult to overcome the sexual jealousy of imagining their partner with another person. Just as hard can be giving a precious child over to the company and influence of that person. It is almost impossible to be objective in these circumstances.

'I'm not letting my child spend time in that trollop's company . . . it'll upset him,' or a version of the same, is the almost universal reaction to this dilemma. What is it the parent is really feeling? Rationally they know that their child is not actually at risk from contact with this person, unless the separation is very new and the child is being pressured into liking someone else too soon. They are saying a combination of things:

> 'I will be upset, not my child, if they meet because I'm insanely jealous of her.'

> 'I am not going to make it easy for my ex-partner to set up a cosy alternative to our relationship. He can have her, but not our child *and* her.'

> 'I am frightened my child will like her better than me and have more fun with her.'

> 'I have lost my partner, I can't lose my child too.'

> 'I hate the thought of her having any influence over my child.'

> 'I'm blaming her because it's easier than blaming my ex-partner.'

Feeling these things is a normal, human reaction to sexual jealousy. Unfortunately the repercussions of these reactions often rebound unfairly on the child, and can create an atmosphere where it is impossible for him to make a relationship with his new step-parent. Now this might be exactly what the parent had in mind, but who will it benefit? Her? Her ex-partner? Her child's step-parent? Her child?

When a couple split up, except in extreme circumstances such as addiction or mental illness, there is responsibility on both sides for what the relationship has become. Someone who becomes involved with a married person is also accountable, but the main responsibility must rest with the two within the marriage. The outsider is more of a symptom than a cause and is often used as a means to avoid facing the problems in the relationship. Whereas recognizing this does not necessarily prevent the marriage from breaking down, it does remove the justification for exclusively demonizing the outsider, and it is this justification which is at the root of much of the negative behaviour relating to step-parents.

'If it wasn't for that bitch we would still be married.'

'She has ruined my marriage and my life.'

'He took her away from me.'

None of the above is helpful when supporting a child as he begins to come to terms with a stepfamily. The child will take on board a parent's emotions and, from feelings of loyalty towards them, will be immediately prejudiced against the new step-parent. Difficult as it is, the adult concerned should try to assign the feelings from the breakdown of her marriage to where they belong, between her and her ex-partner, and not let them spill destructively into the lives around her.

Her confidence destroyed by rejection, it is common for a parent to be fearful that a step-parent will replace her in her child's affection. This is quite unfounded. The child may enjoy the step-parent's company, in fact it is to be hoped he will, in time he may even grow to love his step-parent, but it will neither be the same love, nor in any way competitive with the love he feels for his parent. For the same reason that it is foolish for a step-parent to lay claim to the parenting role, it is also foolish for a parent to be jealous of the step-parenting role. The relationships are quite different and certainly not mutually exclusive.

So a parent must grit her teeth and make every effort to send her child off to his step-parent with reasonably good grace, however difficult this may seem. How does she then cope when he comes back from the weekend and wants to tell her what he's done and what he's eaten and what fun he's had?

* She shouldn't ask too many questions ... she doesn't really want to know.

* She shouldn't sneer at, or criticize, the things he tells her.

* She should be pleased that he has enjoyed himself and not been shouted at, marginalized or abused.

✳ She should try to make him feel comfortable telling her about it. If she doesn't then she won't ever know if he is being shouted at, marginalized or abused.

✳ She should let him know he is allowed to like his step-parent even if it almost kills her to do so.

✳ She should remember that as the resident parent she can make or break her child's step-relationship, and try to make it rather than break it.

The birth-parent in the stepfamily

The parent is the link between her child and her new partner. This pig-in-the-middle situation can be very wearing for her and very unproductive for her family if she insists on trying to act as family go-between and removes the responsibility from their shoulders for making their relationship work. It is best that she discourages them from using her in this way by persuading them to talk directly to each other. If they feel awkward or worried about this initially then she can offer to be there as moral support, but not act as intermediary.

Vanessa remarried when her two girls were twelve and fourteen.

At first I didn't realize they were doing it. Di and Judy would come and complain that they weren't allowed to watch *Neighbours* in the sitting-room now that Peter was working from home, or that he got irritated when they were on the phone for any length of time. These are normal things for a family to argue about, and probably normal for the children to come to their mum for support, but it really wound me up because I felt that the children and Peter didn't understand each other and refused to communicate. When I suggested to the girls they speak directly to their stepfather, they would say: 'You do it, Mum, he'll get cross if we say anything,' which was stupid as he'd never been cross, just firm about things he thought were important. When I asked him to talk directly to the girls instead of whingeing about them to me, he said the same thing: 'Oh, they won't take it from me, you'll have to talk to them.'

I went on acting as pig-in-the-middle for far too long and it was really making me anxious to the point where I found myself watching them all obsessively when we were together and trying constantly to diffuse any potential friction. I began to dread us all being together. I felt so responsible for bringing them together, as if it was my fault, which I suppose it was to some extent. Then one day I just lost it. There had been a problem about the girls coming to Sunday lunch with some friends of Peter's. He wanted them to come, the girls didn't because they didn't know them and didn't see why they should. First I had Peter whingeing on, then the girls separately, and I just exploded. I dragged Peter into the sitting-room, then fetched the girls and shut them all in with instructions not to come out until they had sorted themselves out and found some way to communicate with each other. I also told them I was going out, so that they couldn't all come crying to me. I paced round the park for an hour then gingerly crept back home. There was a real atmosphere and apparently there had been a lot of shouting and crying, but it seems they had confronted each other about all kinds of things, and come to some understanding. There were still problems after that but they began to get on much better and had real rows together, and at least I had removed myself from the line of fire.

It would obviously be less stressful for a parent to try to engineer a degree of communication within her stepfamily earlier than Vanessa did. Having time together, such as meal-times and shared leisure periods, can help make this a natural rather than a manu-factured process. So many members of modern families, both conventional and step, spend their time passing like ships in the night, never making the moment to sit and talk and find out how each other's lives are going. Inevitably this insularity means that people lose touch with those around them, which leads to conflict based on lack of understanding of the other person's agenda. How can a child know why her father keeps shouting if she hasn't been told that he is worried about losing his job? How can a mother appreciate her son's evil mood unless he tells her his girl-friend might be pregnant? It is vital, to achieve harmony in the stepfamily, to persuade them to talk.

Acting as intermediary is not helpful, but it can be equally destructive to a child for a parent not to recognize her role as protector when she brings another adult into the family. Obviously she is keen for her new relationship to work, but she cannot be blind to any injustices her partner might be perpetrating on her child. If her child is being treated unfairly she *must* intervene.

Laura nearly suffered a mental breakdown at the hands of her stepfather, but she has realized since that her mother was as much to blame as her stepfather because she refused to support her.

> I was ten when they married, but Carlo and me never hit
> it off. He was always so critical of me, everything I did
> was wrong, from the way I cleared the breakfast things
> to my weight, my friends, my school work, everything.
> And when he wasn't criticizing me he was ignoring me.
> I would say something at supper and it was as if I hadn't
> spoken . . . but Mum did nothing to defend me. I began to
> feel like an unwelcome guest in my own home. At first
> I blamed him, but she was my mother, she should have
> stuck up for me. I felt so worthless and eventually did the
> predictable and started on drugs, and it wasn't till I took

an overdose that anyone took any notice . . . and even
then Mum just said I was being 'teenagerish'. I realized she
couldn't afford to risk her marriage to Carlo, that she was
prepared to sacrifice me if needs be for her marriage.
I suppose she thought, 'She'll leave home soon anyway and
I'll be left alone, so I have to think of myself,' but I think
that's a terrible way to treat your child. I got therapy,
but me and Mum hardly speak . . . I just can't forgive her
for dumping me like that.

Achieving a balance

It may be difficult at first for a parent in a new stepfamily to find a
balance between the relationship with her child and the relationship with her new partner. It is sensible for her to stick to routines
and ceremonies in the early stages that are important to her
children and to make sure she has plenty of time with them on
their own when they can relax together as a family. If they know
their parent is prepared to make time available to do this,
then they will be more amenable to the time when their step-
parent is also present. Gradually, as they begin to feel more at
home with her partner, this separate time will be less vital, but
still important.

It is a good idea for a parent to explain to her partner before
he moves in that this time alone with her children is precious, but
that it is no reflection on him or his relationship to her children,
and she can then make sure she balances it with time alone
with him. This is often easy to manage when her children visit
their other parent, but if they are not in touch, she could persuade
a relative or friend to have the children for days here and there
so that she and her new partner can sometimes spend parts of
weekends as a couple rather than as a family, and she could also
organize a reliable babysitter for times when they want to go
out in the evening.

Spoiling the child

Yes, it is unfortunate when a relationship breaks down. Yes, the children will have suffered as a result and yes, a parent feels hideously guilty about it. But if he continues to dwell on that guilt he can be in danger of over-compensating his children and so spoiling them. He might then compound this parental guilt by introducing a step-parent into the children's lives, but if a parent continues to indulge his children in the new step-family he will create monsters who will be entirely capable of destroying the relationship between him and his new partner single-handed.

Stewart took on Jemima as a stepdaughter when she was six. Annette, her mother, admitted she was indulgent with her daughter, but Stewart liked Jemima and thought he would be able to deal with it.

At first I suppose I joined in. Whatever Jemima wanted, Jemima got. But after a while it began to really irritate me. If Jemima didn't like the food Annette had cooked, then Annette would go and cook something else for her, leaving our meal to spoil. If Jemima cried and said she didn't want her mother to go out in the evening, then Annette would cancel our outing and stay at home, no matter what our arrangement had been. If Jemima ordered an ice-cream in a restaurant and then wanted another one, Annette would get it for her, despite the fact that the child would then leave half of it. If we were out with friends or family and Jemima said she wanted to go home, then home we'd go. Jemima started to want to sleep in her mother's bed again, which she had done before I arrived, and Annette let her . . . I ended up in Jemima's bed most of the time. I don't know whether I imagined it, but I began to detect a look of triumph on Jemima's face when she won these battles.

> I tried to talk to Annette about it, but she said: 'Look, she's been through such a lot, I owe it to her to spoil her a bit.' It got so that I really hated her. That sounds so awful, for an adult to hate a six-year-old child, but I'm afraid I did, and I began to back off from involving myself with her because I knew if I didn't I would get very angry and I didn't trust myself not to shout, or worse. Then Annette got annoyed with me for not taking more interest in her daughter, and we argued, and the more we argued the more defensive Annette got about Jemima, until the whole thing broke up and I left. Jemima had won, but lost too because she was becoming so unmanageable and tiresome to be with that no one wanted to know her.

Putting a child first is not the same thing as spoiling her. Children need boundaries, they need to know how far is too far, and indulgence born of guilt will do them no favours either now or in the future. A separated parent can deal with her feelings of guilt by accepting them as a normal part of the parenting process, then moving on ... is there a parent alive who doesn't think they could have done a better job in one area or another?

She can talk to her friends, or if necessary a professional counsellor, and get some perspective on her guilt so that she can learn from it, then put it behind her and make the rest of her child's childhood as secure and happy as possible.

Shared parenting

It is easy for a parent to shut her new partner out of the parenting process. Obviously it will take time for a new step-parent and stepchild to adjust to each other, but they will never do so if the parent doesn't allow her partner a role in the stepfamily. It is tempting to fall into the 'guilty' parenting trap discussed earlier, but this 'guilty parenting' is also exclusive parenting; it is saying: 'My child has been through this terrible trauma and now

I will protect her from anything or anyone who might threaten her childhood.' This is fine in theory, she does need her parent's protection, but if that parent has made a careful decision about her new partner's suitability to be part of the family, she must then allow him the chance to become a committed stepfather and not isolate him from the parenting process. A step-parent will need his partner's help in the following areas to ease his path to this goal:

* A parent should let her children know early on that she trusts this person with them and hopes they will trust him too.

* She should let her new partner gradually contribute his own way of doing things to the family structure to accommodate the new mix in the stepfamily.

* The two adults should discuss care of the child together. The step-parent may have no legal rights over his stepchild, but as a step-parent can be helpful and more objective when problems arise. If a parent doesn't allow her new partner to take an interest, he won't.

* It may not be easy to include a step-parent in events involving the child where an ex-partner is present, but the parent should try to find other opportunities to take him along.

* A step-parent coming into a family must tread carefully and avoid criticizing his new partner's parenting skills or dictating any rigid parenting ideals of his own. It is best to see parenting as a joint venture which requires time, support and a lot of careful discussion. The parenting structure which emerges will probably mean compromises and modifications on both sides and a new step-parent must be prepared to be flexible.

To summarize:

* Be sensitive to the trauma your new partner and your stepchild experienced during the family break-up.

* Be flexible about your parenting ideals.

* Don't allow your stepchild to be over-indulged because of your partner's guilt about the family split.

* Don't ask your partner to be pig-in-the-middle. Communicate directly with your stepchild.

* Make sure time with each family member is balanced.

* Be prepared to share the parenting tasks.

* Don't get involved in hostility towards the ex-partner.

CHAPTER 7

Crisis management

So what happens when two adults have created a stepfamily
and it all becomes a disaster, with everyone at each other's throats
and no one knowing who to turn to? There is no need to
panic ... whatever the family is experiencing is quite normal!
This chapter identifies some ways to help resolve the family
conflict.

Communicate

Problems usually occur in life, and especially in families, when
there is a breakdown of communication. Many modern families
spend precious little time actually talking to each other. With the
advent of convenience food and microwave ovens there is not
the expedience there used to be for all the family members to
eat the same thing at the same time. Even if they do all sit down
for a meal there is no guarantee they will talk – they may watch
television instead. So a typical modern family might spend all
week missing any contact with their nearest and dearest beyond:
'Don't forget your packed lunch' ... 'It's your day to go to the
supermarket' ... 'I'm staying over with Jo tonight' ... 'Leave
the money on the hall table' ... 'Pick up Danny, he's on the
six o'clock.' Whereas these exchanges are essential, they don't go
very far in giving an informed picture of each other's lives, so

when tensions arise there is no mechanism in place for dealing with them.

This is never more true than in the early stages of a stepfamily. Divisions may already have been marked off, with the parent and the children in one section, the step-parent and parent in another, so when, for instance, the stepchild leaves his breakfast plate unwashed on the draining-board and goes to school ...

>His stepfather complains to his partner.
>
>She says she will speak to her son.
>
>The son then complains that his stepfather's a tell-tale and a coward for not saying something direct to him.
>
>The mother tells this to the stepfather.
>
>The stepfather is furious at being criticized, and attacks his stepson not just for the dirty plate but for the criticism as well.
>
>The stepson is on the defensive by now and over-reacts to the telling-off.
>
>They both sulk.
>
>The next time there is a need to communicate it is that much more difficult for both of them.

... and all this for a dirty plate. It seems ridiculous, but many people will recognize in this example elements of their own family arguments. To avoid this kind of stalemate keep these things in mind:

* Try to establish a dialogue between all members of the family right from the start. Explain how important it is and why.

* Don't allow any one person to act as family go-between.

* Don't let the sun set on any family conflicts. Resentment breeds resentment.

Identify the problem

Often rows about things like dirty plates are actually due to concealed anger about other unresolved conflicts, the plate just the excuse. In the scenario above perhaps the stepfather was angry that his stepson never accepted discipline from him, or that his partner mollycoddled the boy and always took his side, or that his partner and stepson had different standards of tidiness from his own. Perhaps the stepson resented his stepfather's presence and thought he was being unfairly nagged, or thought his mother wasn't supportive enough of him in the new family set-up. Perhaps the mother felt guilty about bringing her partner into her son's home and was over-compensating. All this unspoken animosity might be hard to voice, so instead they all unconsciously erupt over domestic minutiae. It can be very frightening to admit to, for example, feelings of deep resentment towards a stepchild, or jealousy of a step-parent, especially in the fragile atmosphere of a new stepfamily. Those involved may not even have admitted these feelings to themselves, but not to air the root cause of this anger will result in it being constantly misdirected.

Seize the opportunity to discuss these things when everyone is relaxed and receptive, not just after another argument. Refer to the last few incidents when there has been conflict and ask all the family members to say what they were thinking at the time. Encourage them to be as honest as possible about their feelings, give everyone the chance to have their say without interruptions or recriminations, then discuss what everyone has said as objectively as possible. This may not be easy if problems have been allowed to fester for some time, or if those in the group are not accustomed to airing their feelings, but you should persevere. It may help to bring in an impartial mediator, a relative or friend whom the family really trusts, or if that fails to consider a professional counsellor. An outsider brings a degree of objectivity to the discussions and defuses the intensity of the family group. So, here is a rough guide to identifying the problem:

* Find a quiet time when everyone is relaxed.

* Agree that there is a problem. (This is often the hardest part.)

* Allow all family members to have their say without interruption.

* Discuss what has been said as objectively as possible.

* Don't be afraid to seek outside help if there is no progress – there is no shame in wanting to make a stepfamily work.

The scapegoat

It often happens, in families where there are problems, that one family member in particular becomes the scapegoat and the focus for everyone's anger. Teenagers especially lend themselves to this position because they are stuck inconveniently between childhood and adulthood and can behave in a volatile manner, but any stepchild is at risk from becoming the family scapegoat because she is the one who can be perceived as the odd one out.

The reason a scapegoat is unconsciously adopted in a family is because the other members are unable to voice their negative feelings successfully enough to resolve them. For instance, a stepfather who feels threatened by the relationship between his new partner and his stepchild might focus this insecurity on the stepchild. A mother who still feels rage and humiliation at her ex-partner's desertion might see the child of that union as an unfortunate reminder of her pain. A half-sibling who picks up on his parents' negative feelings might join in the persecution without really knowing the reason for it.

When there are problems in the family which appear to be centred round one family member in particular, it is important to make an honest assessment as to where this antisocial behaviour comes from. It is easy to blame her friends ('a bad influence'), her school ('no discipline'), or the child herself ('she's stupid, selfish, a naughty teenager, takes after her father', etc.), but the child is much more likely to react to the above if she feels isolated and disapproved of at home. The family should talk together to find out how the troublesome member feels and try to own up to any feelings the others may have which unfairly target her as the scapegoat for unresolved family conflict.

Dee lived with her mother, stepfather and two half-siblings from the age of two, but she feels she was always the focus for every-thing that went wrong in the family. She was always shouted at and told she was 'thick and clumsy', always blamed for any row or accident which happened with her half-siblings, always laughed at if she said something that the others didn't agree with.

Of course, after a while I did become stupid and clumsy because I was so scared and felt so worthless. If someone asked me a question I panicked, if I was asked to do any-thing I would rush at it and do it wrong. Mum did try to support me in the early days, but my stepfather was so powerful that she soon gave up and my brothers took the tone from him.

It got so bad that I began to spend all the time at home in my room. My real father hardly saw me because my mother made it so difficult for him . . . punishing him I reckon . . . but in the end he intervened, and when I was nine I went to live with him and my stepmother and their children. I visited my mother still, and as soon as I would step through the door they would start putting me down and criticizing me. My father was much better off than my stepfather and I had nicer clothes and a much happier life, which they all resented of course. But what really

121

shocked me was the first time I went home after I had gone to live with my father. I had a vile evening when they made fun of me and my new lifestyle and viciously criticized my father, and at bedtime my half-brother turned to me and said, 'I'm so glad you're back, Dee, they've been picking on me since you left.' He was only seven.

I blamed myself because everyone else did . . . I still do if anything goes wrong, even as an adult. It's impossible to shake off, despite knowing now that it wasn't anything to do with me, just my stepfather's inadequacy. That's a terrible burden to carry through life.

Ignoring the problem

When everyone is deeply embedded in family conflict it is often hard to draw back sufficiently and recognize that there is something that can be done, and needs to be done. It seems easier to just muddle through with the philosophy that 'it will sort itself out in time'. If the problem is not confronted it certainly will sort itself out in the end, but with what solution? The breakdown of the relationship? A child leaving home too young in order to escape? Someone resorting to Prozac or the local equivalent? These are solutions all right, but not very attractive ones.

Make time, sit down, talk, seek outside help if necessary.

Structured parenting

As discussed earlier on numerous occasions, much of the conflict in a stepfamily is manifested in arguments about parenting, either between children and parents or between the parents themselves. This is common to any family, but particularly so in a stepfamily if the step-parent's role has not been properly defined, or when there is an absent parent who represents a third authority figure for the child outside his resident family. If the parents don't agree on a parenting policy and the parent and step-parent don't agree either, or haven't bothered to discuss it fully, then how will the child know what is expected of him or who he is to heed? If a child's mother says she can't stay out past ten o'clock and her stepfather argues that twelve is more realistic, but when she is with her father he doesn't care if she stays out all night, whose deadline is the child to keep? If a child's mother thinks two pounds pocket money is adequate, his father thinks he should have ten, but won't pay the difference, his stepfather says it's none of his business and they all argue, where does it leave the child? If a child's stepmother thinks she should help with the housework, but her father thinks it's wrong for children to be involved in domestic chores, does she do the housework or not?

The end result of these wrangles is that the child gets blamed for not complying with a very complex set of instructions and philosophies, the child then gets resentful and behaves badly, or plays one parent off against another, the parents then blame each other or him for his behaviour, the tension rises and home life becomes very uncomfortable.

Obviously there will always be differences of opinion about certain events, but parents and step-parents should be able to come to some compromise on the main areas of parenting – discipline, money, education and access to the absent parent – and agree on the role the step-parent will play. Once they have decided on the broad structure they should let the children know what it is, explain their reasons, discuss it if there are objections from older children, then stick to it. Everyone will feel happier if there is a structure to refer back to and from which they can negotiate from time to time.

Some of the main points in a parenting structure for two teenage girls, for instance, might include:

* No going out at night during the school week.

* No smoking in the house.

* Staying out time negotiable, but no later than 1a.m. If the child might be delayed past the curfew she should ring, no matter what the time.

* No boyfriends staying overnight without prior arrangement.

* Visiting with absent parent flexible, but keep everyone informed to avoid double booking.

* Pocket money to be reviewed regularly.

* School work must take precedence over part-time jobs.

The disrupted child

The transition from a family to a stepfamily is a time of huge disruption for a child. He has had to deal not only with the painful period prior to his parents' divorce, when there may have been fights, tension and insecurity, but also with the actual separation and then with the addition of a new authority figure into his family. This authority figure can not only threaten his relationship with his parent, but also finally closes the door on his hopes of parental reunion. The old adage that 'children are so adaptable' is true to some extent, but not for the reasons the adult implies. They are outwardly adaptable because they have to be, they have no choice. This does not mean that the surface acceptance necessary for survival implies that there is any underlying acceptance of the situation in which they find them-selves. Children, like adults, will use the power available to them, which is usually difficult behaviour. They may tell their parent that it is fine for the step-parent to move in because they know this is what their parent wants to hear, but the fact that they are wetting the bed for the first time in years, or having tantrums on the supermarket floor at the age of six, or refusing to do anything their new step-parent suggests, shows that from their point of view it is far from fine.

A parent or step-parent cannot make it fine for their child overnight, but they can understand where the difficult behaviour comes from and be tolerant; they can also explain to the child that they know how hard it must be for him to take a stranger into his family, and that this new adult understands and appreciates his position. Very often all a child wants is acknowledgement of his dilemma and reassurance about what it will mean to him and to his lifestyle. Many parents assume that their child understands what is happening to the family without a careful explanation; he doesn't, and his anxiety at not understanding will make him unhappy and disruptive. Here are a few things to take into account if a child is behaving this way in the new stepfamily:

* He has been traumatized by past, or ongoing, parental discord.

* He doesn't understand what is going to happen to him in the new stepfamily.

* He is finding it difficult to share his parent.

* The loyalty he feels for his absent parent is threatened by a step-parent.

* His hopes of parental reunion are dashed and he most probably blames the step-parent for this.

The adults in a stepfamily should be honest with their child and warn him about any lifestyle changes, be tolerant of his insecurities and give him time to adjust.

Believing in the stepfamily

Divorced parents and stepchildren are often under the illusion that all families that stay together are perfectly and blissfully happy twenty-four hours a day. This is ridiculous. Stepfamilies can be just as happy as any other family; what causes conflict in all families is lack of communication and the inability to be honest about feelings, not the genetic relationship between the individual members. To establish a good rapport in a stepfamily can take a bit of effort on everyone's part, but the members of a stepfamily will never make it work if they take the basic attitude that stepfamilies are second best. They should not just focus on the problem areas in the family, but should congratulate themselves on the successful areas too. For instance, a person might have recently become a step-parent and be finding it harder than he thought, sometimes resenting the effort involved in caring for his stepchild and wishing she would just disappear ... that's the bad part. The good part is that, in fact, he actually likes and respects his stepchild and she seems to like him, and he loves his partner and is very committed to the relationship. The bad part is normal and needn't be a cause for too much angst. Step-relationships take a long time to mature and as long as everyone is communicating with each other and discussing why they sometimes wind each other up, they will find things gradually settle down. And remember, there is no such thing as a perfect family.

Vicky found her eleven-year-old stepdaughter a nightmare at first ... moods, sulks, insolence, despite all her efforts to make her feel at home.

> She had been with us full-time for nearly a year and, although things were a lot easier than at the beginning, she still seemed to have these terrible moods all the time and refuse to do what I said. Barry was no help because he was away all the time, which of course added to my resentment. In the end I decided to see a counsellor. We all went and sat there, feeling foolish, and I told him that I didn't think it was working and that Ginny seemed to hate me, Barry didn't help me with her and that I was at my wits' end. The counsellor then asked Ginny if she hated

me and why she had the moods and was so uncooperative. Ginny said she didn't hate me at all but she felt she was a burden to me and that her parents had both let her down and she didn't feel she could trust anyone, in fact that I was the only person who really seemed to care and that she hated her moods as much as I did but couldn't seem to control them. I was amazed, and really touched.

The counsellor said we were basically doing fine after such a short time together and that I should be less hard on myself because I was doing a good job. It made Barry sit up and take notice too, which was great, and he apologized for not being more attentive to Ginny. All in all it was the most productive hour we have ever spent, and after that, because we'd all aired our feelings and been told we were doing OK, things slowly got a lot better.

Professional help

As the last example demonstrates, this can be the jolt everyone needs. Many people are very wary of what they think counsellors represent, imagining weeks of uncomfortably angst-ridden sessions which require everyone to bare their souls. It is more constructive to try to see counsellors as facilitators, as people who are there to help the family clarify their feelings in an objective, detached fashion. Talking to friends is also important and helpful, particularly to vent a particular frustration or share experiences, but a counsellor is not going to be at the same party the following week, and it is unlikely that the family members concerned will bump into her outside the school or the supermarket, or share an office with her, so everyone can feel safe to say what they like, however unacceptable they may think it to be.

Seeking professional help is not a sign of failure. The 'I should be able to sort this out myself' syndrome only adds stress and anxiety to an already difficult situation. Everyone needs help with step-parenting, it is universally acknowledged as a very complex arena, but professional counsellors often bemoan the fact that families leave it too late before seeking help, when the rift between the family members has gone beyond the point of no return; things have been said which can't be forgotten, things done which can't be forgiven. It is advisable not to let the family problems escalate to this point. Parents and step-parents can contact local or national organizations such as the National Stepfamily Association in Britain, or see their doctor for referral to a suitable counsellor. (See the directory at the back of this book.)

A shared experience

Every stepfamily thinks their problems are unique. They very rarely are: disliking a stepchild, disliking a step-parent, disliking the fact that a partner and child dislike each other … these are all horribly normal. Stepfamily members should talk to others in a similar boat to themselves, or join a local step-parenting group – people will be only too happy to share their experiences with them.

It takes time

For those who have read the rest of this book this will be a boring refrain, but it's true, stepfamilies take time to come together successfully, and 'time' means years, not weeks or months. It is important for the stepfamily members to be aware of the trigger points listed below and not be too hard on themselves when things aren't immediately perfect. They should also recognize and accept that there may be problems in the early stages and try to have a sense of humour about them … they are probably doing fine.

List of trigger points to guard against

* Attempting to create a stepfamily too soon.

* Disrespect for the absent parent. No child can stand to hear his parents unfairly criticized.

* The 'Call me Dad' syndrome – step-parents trying to replace the absent parent in their stepchild's affection.

* Lack of communication in the family.

* Brushing family problems under the carpet and not making time to sort them out.

* Scapegoating one family member.

* Not having enough separate time for parent/child, parent/partner relationships.

* Imposing new parenting rules and lifestyle on a stepchild too soon.

* Disagreeing about a parenting structure.

* Not preparing a child sufficiently for the birth of half-siblings.

* Discriminatory treatment of half- and step-siblings.

* Not supporting the existing child in the new stepfamily.

* Allowing guilt about the family break-up to affect the way a person parents their child.

* Lying to a child (about anything).

* Not keeping a child informed about changes in his lifestyle.

* Cutting off the children from an ex-partner's extended family (i.e. Gran).

* Leaving it too late to seek outside help when things go wrong.

And remember:

* There's no such thing as failure, just problems and solutions.

* There are thousands of stepfamilies out there who share these problems.

* Stepfamilies take a *long time* to become successful.

* Stepfamilies can be just as happy as conventional families in time.

* There is no need to panic.

CHAPTER 8

Support systems

Everyone needs friends and family to help them through their lives, share their experiences, both good and bad, and support them when things go wrong. This is never more true than for the members of a stepfamily. The trouble is that when an adult and parent survives a family breakdown, then embarks on a new relationship which becomes a stepfamily, they will have invested an enormous amount in the success of this new venture, and as a result may think that any problems and conflicts they have will be seen as another failure by those around them. This perception might make them reluctant to ask for help from the people closest to them, for fear those concerned will shake their heads and mutter: 'Here we go again.' Likewise a step-parent, perhaps unaware of some of the common pitfalls of step-parenting, may think that the problems he faces are unique to him and his stepfamily and so be ashamed to admit to what he also perceives as failure.

It is vital that the adults in a stepfamily do not cut themselves off from the support of friends and family. This is when they most need the encouragement and assistance of those they love and trust. If they isolate themselves from this source of help they will only increase their stress and sense of isolation.

Parents, grandparents, siblings, aunts, uncles and cousins can be enormously supportive of a stepfamily. They can offer a mediating voice, a shoulder to cry on, a breather from problems within the stepfamily and a haven for a bewildered child. They can also offer the sense of a wider belonging so often missing in the early stages of a stepfamily. Sadly they are often forgotten in the trauma of a family rift and their support is marginalized or ignored.

Losing the extended family

When a couple separates it is almost inevitable that, if sides are taken, the extended family will stick with its own; anything less might be seen as rank disloyalty. This position can affect everyone involved, but as usual the implications of side-taking can rebound most heavily on the children. A much-loved grand-parent can be a source of great comfort and support when a child's parents are at each other's throats, she can offer a haven of constancy and normality when the child feels the rest of his world is falling apart, but once a couple split up, it is sometimes harder for the grandparents of the non-resident parent to keep in touch. They may feel disinclined, out of a sense of family loyalty, to continue their relationship with their daughter- or son-in-law if the split has been acrimonious, or they may be rejected in their requests for a visit with their grandchildren on purely punitive grounds. This is also true of aunts, uncles and cousins. Grand-parents now have the right to seek contact with their grand-children, but enforcing this can take stamina and determination.

Peter was ten when his parents divorced:

> They only left each other when Dad fell in love with some-one at work, but they had been at each other's throats for years . . . for ever in fact. Gramma, Dad's mum, lived a couple of streets away, and whenever I saw a row coming on I'd make some excuse to see how she was and go and hide there till I thought they'd have finished. Gramma would then ring them and see if they sounded normal, and

if they did I'd go home. She was my salvation. When Dad left Mum Gramma was very angry with him, and with Mum, she said they were like a couple of children, and she never really took sides, but Mum thought she was bound to side with Dad and put her in the enemy camp. Not long after Dad left she forbade me to go and see her, saying she was a 'spy'. I was devastated, Gramma was the only proper adult in my life. Mum would yell at me every time I went out to play: 'Don't you go near that woman . . . ' I didn't at first, but then I bumped into her in the shop and we made a pact that I would pop round if I thought it safe . . . such ridiculous cloak and dagger stuff for a visit to my grandmother, eh? Of course Mum found out, I think Dad told her, but in the end I think she realized she couldn't stop me. I couldn't have survived my childhood without Gramma's common sense and love.

Parents and step-parents should try to encourage contact with any members of their ex-partner's family with whom their child has a close relationship, be they grandparents, aunts, uncles or cousins. It may not be easy at first, but if they can make sure that any marital strife is kept between them and their ex-partner and not allowed to spill into other family relationships, they stand a better chance. The child's grandparents and other relatives will be just as keen to maintain contact as the child is, and can be a great help to the parents and step-parents in caring for the child at a difficult time, for instance allowing the new couple to spend some time on their own without the children.

Recreating the extended family

One of the problems a stepfamily can face is isolation from the usual family rituals associated with engagement, marriage, childbirth, wedding anniversaries, etc. There may be less enthusiasm or endorsement from the extended family members for the new relationship and an awkwardness about how to treat the step-relations, not to mention the scars from the original family rift centred around loyalty to the previous partner. But these rituals are important, as they reinforce a sense of the extended family, allowing families with busy lives a moment to remember where they come from and to whom they belong.

Any initial awkwardness on the part of the extended family is perhaps understandable because in a stepfamily this sense of belonging can be muddied. A family reunion is only 'family' for some of the members, and it is sometimes hard for a step-parent to persuade his extended family to take on his stepchildren as their own in the same way that he has. This lack of acceptance can be borne out in small, but nonetheless hurtful, ways such as discrimination with half-siblings about birthday and Christmas presents, holiday visits and treats, and can reinforce a stepchild's sense of isolation in his new stepfamily.

A new stepfamily can try to engender a sense of the wider family from the start by including other family members in parties and special occasions such as birthdays and anniversaries and by insisting that any step-relation treats all the children in the stepfamily fairly. If a brother is giving a present to his niece, he must be persuaded to give one to his step-niece also. If a mother and father want to take their grandchild to the cinema, they must ask their stepgrandchild to come too. It is important for a step-parent to include a stepchild on Christmas cards to his relatives, to include her when his relatives ring to ask about the family, to take her with him when he visits his family for Sunday lunch. Unless his stepchild is a two-headed monster, his extended family will soon accept her in the way he has, and she will accept them.

Personal support

Even for those who are communicating within their stepfamily and doing their best to make things run smoothly, it is important to have the support of friends or siblings outside the immediate family to whom the parents and step-parents can vent their frustrations. However good a step-parent's relationship with her stepdaughter is, for example, she may still find her maddening at times, but would prefer not to criticize her endlessly to her father. The step-parent should not be ashamed of these feelings, and it helps to find a friend who understands that her carping and irritation is just letting off steam and knows that discussing her stepchild's behaviour and perhaps laughing about it can help her to return to the family with renewed tolerance and humour. It is even better if she can find someone in the same position as herself, who understands the particular emotions involved in stepfamilies and will not be shocked or pejorative about her harmless rantings.

Support groups and associations

Outside the family there are now many support groups where the members of a stepfamily can go to share experiences and talk through their problems. These groups can help them realize that they are not alone, that any frustrations they may have are entirely normal, and can help to put some perspective on their situation. They will be able to put the step-parent or parent in touch with a trained counsellor, who can discuss any problems related to the stepfamily, and also make available leaflets and publications dealing with every aspect of stepfamily life, including, for example, residence orders, adoption, finance, legislation which relates to the stepfamily, child abuse. Information about these groups can be found in local libraries or health centres. (See also the directory at the back of this book.)

Family therapy

If things are going wrong in the stepfamily and the adults involved feel they need professional help, it is a good idea to consider family therapy. Until recently, therapy has had rather a precious image ... angst-ridden media stars and troubled creative geniuses in the Woody Allen mould. It was seen as an American indulgence that the British were both suspicious of, and too sane to require – the Brits, after all, have a stiff upper lip. However, it has now become a much more accepted approach when people find themselves facing periods in their lives when things are confusing and frightening.

Family therapy, as opposed to individual therapy, is particularly helpful for a family with problems, because it brings everyone together, instead of dealing with each unit separately. It gives each family member the chance to air their views to the other members, but within the safety of the counselling room. Very often all that the family needs is the reassurance that they are doing fine, but if there are more serious underlying factors then they can be brought out into the open and discussed with the aid of a trained professional.

The adults in the stepfamily should not see therapy as a last resort or as a resort exclusively for the 'mad'; the therapist is there to facilitate safe discussion and perhaps iron out a few simple problems which have been causing disproportionate trouble because they have not been dealt with in the family group. She is trained to see through, for example, the argument about the dirty plates mentioned in an earlier chapter, and focus on what this argument actually represents. She will be able to look at the inter-action between all the family members and offer an objective opinion about what she sees, but she will not either judge them or blame them for it. Even if it sounds frightening to air intimate family problems with a stranger, they should remember that the therapist is used to it, it is her job. What they are saying will probably come as no surprise to her, and there is some comfort in recognizing this.

Supporting each other

Obviously the first line of support in the stepfamily should be each other, but it is easy in a stepfamily to allow the children to drive a wedge between the adults. For reasons of insecurity a child might cling unnaturally close to his parent when a new adult takes up residence, and the parent may indulge this at first. However, if the child gets into the habit of always getting his own way and receiving immediate attention to his every whim, it is likely that the adults will begin to fall out over the spoilt child. Some children may even manipulate this situation deliberately.

The adults in the stepfamily should support each other in a joint parenting venture and not throw blame about without reason. They should try to be objective about the child's real needs, have plenty of time alone together when they aren't both tired and stressed from work, and occasionally spoil themselves, not just the children.

The ex-partner's support

There will be some people who mutter, 'In your dreams', at the suggestion of support from the ex-partner, and perhaps in some cases they will be right, but it must be true that if two people have once got on well enough to marry each other and have children together, if they make sufficient effort to get on after the separation, it will happen. Genuine friendship is unrealistic in many cases, so people in this position should aim for a practical, working relationship. Perhaps this will not come about at first, it might take a few years of forced politeness and gritted teeth, but it seems ridiculous that people can still have the energy to fight with each other twenty and thirty years after the event. There are cases of divorced couples who have taken more than ten years just to reach a divorce settlement. This seems a terrific waste of time. A couple should start as they mean to go on, purely for the children's sake if necessary, by building a working relationship which can last throughout their childhood, even through a stepfamily. It won't be for ever – children, unlike pets, grow up eventually.

Financial support in the stepfamily

This is a knotty problem! Money is obviously one of the main areas of conflict, after the children, when it comes to divorce and remarriage, and there is no easy answer. If, after divorce, it were simply a matter of the two separated adults making sure that each had enough to live on and support the children, then conflict in this arena would be a thing of the past ... but it is not. Money is also guilt, money is also a measure of worth, money is also a weapon, money is also a bribe, money is also a substitute for love, money is control. Some of these sentiments will be very familiar to separated parents and their partners.

> 'I'm giving her everything, it's the least I can do.'

> 'He thinks I'm worth twelve thousand a year after all I've done for him? Washing his shirts, cooking his ghastly business dinners ...'

> 'She won't argue, not with all the money I'm giving her.'

> 'He thinks I care about the money, I just want him back.'

> 'I'm not giving her money so that lout can sponge off me.'

> 'I'll take him for all he's worth.'

These statements appear, on the surface, to be about money, but in fact they are about a complicated set of emotions, so when one family is breaking down and another being formed, the financial arrangements can become very complex. How can the adults

involved make sure this doesn't happen? The only way is to resolve
as best they can the conflict between them and their ex-partner.
If a woman is angry and hurt at her partner's desertion then she
must talk her feelings out with him, tell him how she feels, try to
understand why he behaved the way he did, and only after both
sides have taken the time to do this should they discuss their
financial position. It is often hard to persuade the partner who has
been the one to leave the relationship to have this heart-to-heart.
They may think it simpler just to run and distance themselves
from the trauma of facing up to each other's pain. In the short
term this may be so, but in the long term it will cause bitterness
and confusion for everyone concerned, particularly when practical
arrangements such as finance have to be considered. It is only
when a separated couple have some understanding of each other's
position that they can put money back where it ought to be,
i.e. a means of paying for their own and their children's lifestyle.
The new emphasis on settlements out of court with regard to
money and property helps towards avoiding the bitter and expensive repercussions of lawyers fighting lawyers to no one's benefit
except their own.

The step-parent's financial commitment

The financial support of a full-time step-parent for his stepchild
can not easily be delineated. The absent father will be responsible
for maintenance until the child is eighteen, and this should
cover her living expenses, but who pays for holidays? Who pays
for treats? Who pays for the child's bedroom to be redecorated?
Who pays for driving lessons? Regardless of the amount of money
available for these things, conflict and resentment can result if
there is tension between the stepfamily and the absent parent or
between the step-parent and the stepchild. Providing money, or
refusing it, can then be used as a means of control or to play
out emotional dissonance, supplying a perfect cover for the real

problems. So the adults in the stepfamily should face up to conflicts within the family and try to resolve them without letting money arguments act as the beard. It is best for those concerned to work out how they are going to manage their finances as a stepfamily right from the start, so that there is as little ambiguity as possible. This includes making a solid arrangement about maintenance with the ex-partner so that everyone knows where they stand.

Collecting the maintenance

Another problem surrounding money arises if there is difficulty making the absent partner keep to his commitment. If the reason the maintenance is irregular or actually withheld is to do with emotional conflict and not genuine hardship, then it makes sense for the adults involved to try to sort this out between them, perhaps with an independent arbitrator if they don't feel they can do this without destructive rows.

Financial inequality

When there is a large discrepancy between the income of the absent parent and the income of the full-time step-parent, inequalities can be created between the stepchild and birth-children of the stepfamily. For instance, take a situation where the absent parent is very rich and can afford to buy top-of-the-range trainers for his child, but the step-parent is in a more restricted financial position and the other children have to make do with cheaper ones. These cheaper trainers would not be a problem for the children except that they are comparing them with their half-sister's state-of-the-art pair. This can cause resentment between siblings and between step-parent and stepchild. Equally the reverse can be true, where the step-parent is rich but the absent parent is less well-off, with the result, if the step-parent chooses to be discriminatory, that the birth-children in the stepfamily have ponies and private schools, but the stepchild does not. Children have to accept the reality of economic inequality at some stage, and an absent parent has the right to buy the trainers he thinks are the best for his child as long as he is not doing it out of a desire to compete with the step-parent for his child's love, and as long as he is not indulging in guilty parenting. If all the children in the stepfamily are treated the same and completely fairly in every way, then the trainers will not become an issue either for the birth-child or the stepchild.

Here are a few things for the adults to remember when dealing with financial matters within the stepfamily:

* Money can represent more than just financial support – for example, guilt, a measure of worth, bribery or control.

* Settled relationships usually mean settled financial commitments.

* Fair and equal treatment of all the children in the family is vital.

Inheritance

Another knotty problem! This is obviously a matter for the individual, but a step-parent should remember that stepchildren will not automatically inherit from his estate unless he makes specific provision for them in his will. If a step-parent adopts his stepchildren then they will be in the same position as the birth-children. Many stepchildren who have been close to their step-parents are very hurt by their step-parent's unintentional omission in this respect.

To summarize:

A stepfamily, like any other family, needs a great deal of support, so it is best for those involved to remember:

* Not to shut their nearest and dearest out when they have problems. Everyone has problems of one sort or another, at one time or another.

* Not to lose the extended family because of petty side-taking or residual bitterness. It can be a great help.

* To involve the extended stepfamily right from the start and make sure they treat all the children in the stepfamily the same.

* To have a friend to whom they can let off steam about their problems.

* To make use of local stepfamily support groups, counsellors and stepfamily literature.

* Not to be afraid of family therapy if things are out of control.

* To make sure they support each other and don't give all the treats to the children.

* To make sure that the parent has the support of the ex-partner.

* To sort out finance, to decide on step-parent commitment, to regularize maintenance, to treat all children financially fairly.

* Not to forget their will.

CHAPTER 9

Conclusion:
Stepfamilies *can* work

It is important first to debunk the myth that stepfamilies don't
work because they are stepfamilies and therefore second best.
Some don't, it's true, but there are also many conventional families
who have problems. Violence, child abuse, alienation, financial
problems ... these are not the exclusive preserve of any one social
bracket, any one sex, any one nationality, any one particular
type of family. Research is so far limited regarding the function-
ing stepfamily, a situation which is slowly improving, and the
research to date, mostly gleaned from families already identified
as 'at risk' for reasons of social inadequacy, substance addiction,
criminality or mental illness, offers a frightening picture of
violence and abuse perpetrated on stepchildren by their stepfathers. This is the negative, alarmist image of stepfamilies
presented by the media, which is really the only image we have,
apart from the 'wicked stepmother' leering from the pages of
fairy-tales and fiction long before the word 'media' was invented
in its current form. There are, unfortunately, no articles or television programmes about successful stepfamilies. As the number
of stepfamilies increases, it is to be hoped that this negative
image will be balanced by more research, support and acceptance, because blood relatives are not the only people who
can successfully raise a child.

Stepfamilies *are* different

To pretend that stepfamilies are the same as conventional families is to tap into the fear that 'different' is necessarily worse. It is the same fear that says that mothers are always better than fathers at raising children, because mothers have traditionally taken on the main parenting role in our society. Stepfamilies are badly served by not acknowledging the differences, and this denial can be the source of many of the problems the stepfamily faces. For instance:

    ✻ If a step-parent pretends he is a child's father the child will resent it, the step-parent will know it isn't true and the relationship will be based on lies. What is wrong with being a *step*father?

    ✻ Love and a sense of responsibility grow slowly and naturally for a birth-child; a step-parent has to learn these things for his stepchild.

    ✻ Stepfamilies take time to settle down and can't be hurried.

    ✻ The first family will always be there.

    ✻ Unresolved feelings of failure, bitterness, rejection and insecurity from the previous relationship can undermine a stepfamily without the participants being aware of the source of the problem.

Acknowledging these differences should provide understanding and awareness in the stepfamily, not be a source of defeatism that they can never be a 'conventional' family. In fact the sooner the pundits stop harking back to some mythical golden age when everyone's family life was blissfully happy and children spent long sun-soaked days with ginger-beer-and-boiled-egg picnics and parents who drank Ovaltine and listened to soothing bedtime stories on the wireless, the better. According to these pundits the reasons for the demise of The Family vary; everything is blamed from contraception, feminism, liberal divorce laws, microwaves, to unemployment, the War, the discontinuation of conscription, the sixties, but if this is so and families in the past were relentlessly happy and conventional, how do we account for the vast canon of literature stretching back over the centuries which tells us differently? From the Bible, through Chaucer, Shakespeare, Fielding, Austen, Dickens, George Eliot, Ford Madox Ford, Hardy, Ibsen and Chekhov (I could go on for ever), literature has been using what we would now term 'disfunctional' families as fodder for their drama. Let's face it, families have always had the potential for conflict and disaster. Hamlet's family wasn't disfunctional because his mum was on the Pill or the divorce laws were too liberal, Anna Karenina didn't leave her husband and child because she was a feminist ... so we should stop buying into this myth of the 'perfect' family. It has never existed and probably never will.

To use Bruno Bettelheim's phrase, we have 'good enough' families, and these can be stepfamilies just as much as what we like to call 'conventional' families. As long as a family represents love, nurturing, respect and security for its members, it does not matter whether the ties are those of blood or those of inclination, and today's family is as varied and eccentric as it has always been, it's just that now we have labels, moralizing, political capital, the media spotlight, marketing and law to define it. So, even though the stepfamily may be 'different' from what people have been conditioned to consider the 'norm' ... members of a stepfamily must, themselves, believe in it.

So ... suppose the members of a new stepfamily do believe in the concept of a successful stepfamily, but are nervous as to how to achieve it. How can they give themselves the best opportunity for success? There are four main categories to consider for anyone embarking on a stepfamily: responsibility, respect, communication and support.

Responsibility

A stepfamily needs to recognize the responsibility involved in creating a new family. It is not a commitment to be entered into lightly. However, if it is a carefully considered decision on both sides, made over time, there is no reason why it cannot work. Children are traumatized by the breakdown of a family, that is a fact, but if the parent and step-parent present a consistent, secure and loving lifestyle for them, and continue to encourage close contact with the absent parent, the children will survive and possibly take strength from that survival which will stand them in good stead in later life.

The adults in a stepfamily must be responsible enough to realize when there are problems, and face up to them.

Obviously it is a parent's responsibility to protect their child as much as possible by avoiding the introduction of another adult into their life who might cause them harm, emotionally or physically. This cannot be stressed enough. But they also have a responsibility to themselves. If they collapse, nobody will benefit. So it is important that they are kind to themselves and don't waste valuable energy on guilt and remorse. If and when they do decide that it is time to make their family into a stepfamily, then they have the responsibility not to go into the commitment lightly. This certainly does not mean forgoing relationships, but it is better not to bring them into the home until the adults concerned are as convinced as they can be that the relationship has long-standing potential. They should then take their time.

Respect

A stepfamily needs to respect itself and the individual members therein. Everyone will be familiar with parents who say things to their children that they would never dream of saying to a friend or even a passing acquaintance, even if they were true. Things like: 'Look what you've done now, you stupid girl, you're so clumsy,' or 'Of course Debbie's not like Michael, he's got all the brains,' or 'You've got such a fat bottom,' or 'Do they really want you as the lead in the school play?' Put-downs, things said either directly to a child or in their hearing that are believed by the child and help to create a low self-esteem. Often parents say these things because they are insecure themselves and thus about their children, but it is finally a lack of respect, an inability to see a child as a person deserving of respect, for the mere fact that he is a child. There is a difference between necessary discipline and disrespect. It is all right to say to a small child, 'Don't touch the teapot, it's hot and you'll burn yourself,' but not all right to say 'You're so stupid, I can't trust you with anything, even an idiot would know the teapot is hot.' Both reprimands will stop the child touching the teapot for the time being, but the latter will make the child feel guilty, stupid and inadequate into the bargain.

Most people will also no doubt be familiar with the same lack of respect between one adult and another and therefore from child to adult ... a child learns very quickly. This disrespect is often passed off as 'honesty', but really it is a person trampling on another person's psyche, perhaps because their own has been trampled on in the same way in their childhood. Whereas repressing feelings within a family is not a good idea, neither is treating the other members of the family as if their feelings don't count. Children are very impressionable, and if a parent or step-parent constantly mocks them or their partner, constantly points out their weaknesses and laughs at their mistakes, never listens to them or gives them the benefit of the doubt, they will grow up cruel and mocking too. This is never more true than when dealing with the insecurities inherent in a stepfamily, so the adults in a stepfamily should think before they speak and show their partner and children some respect. They, in turn, will be respected.

This respect should also extend to the absent parent. It often seems easier to fight, easier to retain the hatred and bitterness, easier to maintain a position of sinned against or sinner, because to do otherwise involves time and effort and, horror of horrors, seeing the other person's point of view. In fact those who consider that a degree of reconciliation is harder than the habit of aggression are deluding themselves. Ongoing fights, manipulations, game playing and bitterness take up an enormous amount of energy ... much, much more than the exertion required to come to a practical, working arrangement with an ex-partner. There is no requirement for those involved actually to like each other, just to offer each other a degree of respect.

Communication

A stepfamily must communicate, otherwise jealousies and resentments build up, and what started off as a minor paranoia about a misunderstood comment becomes a major hate campaign fuelled by scores of innocent remarks, looks, gestures and perceived unfairness. This is not an exaggeration – there are millions of stepchildren out there who spent a large amount of their childhood in a seething mass of resentment and hatred for their parental figures, just because they felt they were not listened to, felt they were not allowed to express their feelings, and saw discrimination in every parental breath. Some of their tales will be true, but it is certain that plenty more were the paranoid exaggerations of a child who feels he has no voice.

A step-parent, equally, can feel very excluded and superfluous; he can feel that his opinions are ignored, his authority thwarted, and that, like the child, he has no voice. A parent can become the unwilling mediator between her partner and her child. This can all be easily overcome by communication. One family employed what they referred to as 'moaning minutes'. This was five minutes each, uninterrupted, every week, when they could take it in turns to say exactly what they liked about what had gone on in the family that week. They said it cleared the air, that because everyone knew they would have that time, they didn't get frustrated with each other to the same extent, and that the moans which came up had to be dealt with; if they weren't then they came up again the next week with renewed force. However a stepfamily decides to deal with family moans, it is best to make sure they do it all together, and not in secretive huddles which can become divisive and bitchy before long.

Support

A stepfamily needs support. It is a good idea to involve the extended families and friends in a stepfamily venture, to let them know how serious the commitment is and to encourage them to join in. The adults in a stepfamily shouldn't be shy of seeking professional help if they feel things are getting out of control, or of taking advantage of support groups where they can share their experiences with others in the same boat. Above all, they should seek support from the members of the stepfamily itself, letting each member know that the new stepfamily is a joint venture and that close collaboration with each other is essential. Very often a child sees a stepfamily as merely an adult convenience, and the new step-parent sees the stepfamily as a relationship commitment, but not a parental one. To be successful each member has to feel an essential part of the stepfamily.

Love

The word 'love' has been mostly avoided in this book, because it tends to engender panic in the members of a stepfamily. 'Do I love my stepchild as much as my own children?' 'Should I love my stepchildren as much or in the same way as my own children?' 'Why doesn't he love my child as much as our children?' 'Why doesn't she love me as much as she loves her own children?'

'Can step-parental love be the same as birth-parental love?' and so on. The answer to all these questions is that 'love' takes many different forms and no one form is essentially better than another. Thinking briefly of the members of a family, it can be recognized that most people have different degrees of love for, say, a mother, an aunt, a grandmother, a nephew and a child. This does not mean that any of those degrees of love are invalidated by the others. The problem comes when expectations dictate that a step-parent should love his stepchild, and vice versa, quickly, automatically and to the same degree as he does his own child or his parent. They won't, but it is to be hoped that they will eventually forge a kind of love which suits them both and is not denigrated by comparison.

What a step-relationship means to those involved inevitably varies. A step-parent who takes on a small stepbaby will have the time and opportunity that a birth-parent has to grow very close to his stepchild, but a step-parent who takes on a child who is already a teenager will probably never forge such a close bond, and neither he nor his stepchild will expect to. Step-people should not be told how they feel or how they ought to feel about their step-relations. This is a personal thing between individual step-children and step-parents, and they should be allowed to find their own level and take their own time – there are no rules.

So what is a step-parent to his stepchild? Is he an uncle? Is she a sister? Is she a friend? Is he a godfather? Although there are echoes of all these relationships, a step-parent is really none of them: it is an unique relationship, and at its best a very mutually satisfying one. There is the closeness of the family tie, the familiarity which is exclusive to home, yet there are none of the constraints of family. A step-parent can have an objectivity which a parent often lacks, but an involvement which is still supportive, and because of the effort both the step-parent and the stepchild have put into their relationship to make it successful there can be huge gratification at a successful outcome.

There can be real advantages to having a step-parent. With a step-parent a child can be free from onerous parental expectations, free from judgemental parenting, free from the nightmare of the 'child as reflection of parent' syndrome, and free from unfortunate comparisons with ex-partners. These freedoms can be of considerable value, especially during teenage years when there is benefit to be gleaned from having a mediating ally in the adult camp.

So everyone involved in a stepfamily should enjoy it for what it is. No one should be dismayed by the potential problems outlined in this book; whatever they might be, it is usually possible to solve them with a little care and consideration ... and it is well worth the effort. Our stepfamily has had numerous dramas, plenty of rows, much despair, family therapy, hard work and countless readjustments for us all over the seventeen years since its creation. We have made lots of mistakes, but we are now very much an integrated family. We still have rows, of course, but the rows are of the routine variety common to families up and down the land and not related to the fact that we are a stepfamily. My stepdaughter has tested me, driven me mad, taught me a lot about myself, as children always do, and, dare I say it? I love her.

To summarize finally:

Time
* Stepfamilies take time, lots of time, lots and lots of time, but they are worth every minute of the effort put into them.

Responsibility
* A parent and step-parent are both responsible for a child's safety and happiness.

* In order to look after a child a person must also be kind to themselves and get the help they need. It is never helpful to indulge in pointless guilt or blame.

✻ A child needs both parents, so the adults in a step-family and the absent parent should facilitate the child keeping in touch.

Respect
✻ The adults in a stepfamily should try to foster a modicum of respect for an ex-partner, for the child's sake. If this is the only message the reader takes away from this book then it will have been worthwhile!

✻ The adults in a stepfamily should respect themselves, each other and their child.

Communication
✻ No one should ever let problems fester. The members of a stepfamily should make opportunities to talk to each other and listen to what the others are saying.

Support
✻ It is vital not to isolate the stepfamily from those who might help, be it friends, extended family, support agencies or counsellors.

Faith
✻ Members of a stepfamily must have faith.

Good luck!

Bibliography and further reading

Tobe Aleksander, *His, Hers, Theirs: a financial handbook for stepfamilies*, Stepfamily Publications, 1995.

Batchelor, Dimmock and Smith, *Understanding Stepfamilies*, Stepfamily Publications, 1994.

Bruno Bettelheim, *The Good Enough Parent*, Thames & Hudson, 1987.

Bruno Bettelheim, *Survival*, Thames & Hudson, 1979.

John Bowlby, *Attachment and Loss*, 3 vols, Hogarth Press, 1969, 1973, 1980; Penguin, 1980.

John Bowlby, *Child Care and the Growth of Love*, Penguin, 1965.

Anne Charlish, *Caught in the Middle*, Ward Lock, 1997.

Bernadine Coverley, *Successful Step-parenting*, Bloomsbury, 1996.

Erica De'ath, *Stepfamilies, What do we know? What do we need to know?* Stepfamily Publications, 1992.

Alice Miller, *Breaking the Wall of Silence, to join the waiting child*, Virago, 1991.

A. Mitchell, *Children in the Middle*, Tavistock, 1985.

Judith Wallerstein and Joan Kelly, *Surviving the Break-up: How Parents and Children Cope with Divorce*, Basic Books, New York, 1980.

Useful addresses

UNITED KINGDOM

**British Association
of Counselling**
1 Regent Place
Rugby
Warwickshire
CV21 2PJ
Tel: 01788 578328
Keeps a register of approved
counsellors.

Children's Legal Centre
University of Essex
Wivenhoe Park
Colchester
Essex
C04 3SQ
Helpline: 01206 873820
Gives advice on law and policy
affecting children and young
people.

Families Need Fathers
BM Families
London
WC1N 3XX

Helpline: 0181 886 0970
Advice, support and
representation for parents
following separation and
divorce.

Family Helpline
01574 260206
Source of information, referrals
to other agencies and helpline if
you have a problem and need
someone to talk to.

Gingerbread
16–17 Clerkenwell Close
London
EC1R 0AA
Tel: 0171 336 8184
Support for lone parents and
their families.

Helpline for Men
0181 644 9914
Dealing with domestic
violence.

London Marriage Guidance Council
76a New Cavendish Street
London
W1M 7LB
Tel: 0171 580 1087

National Council for One Parent Families
255 Kentish Town Road
London
NW5 2LX
Tel: 0171 267 1361

National Family Mediation
9 Tavistock Place
London
WC1H 9SN
Tel: 0171 383 5993
Fax: 0171 383 5994

NSPCC (National Society for the Prevention of Cruelty to Children)
67 Saffron Hill
London
EC1N 8RS
Tel: 0171 825 2500
Family centres and advocacy for children, work with survivors and perpetrators of abuse, helplines, training for listening to children and preparation for parenthood.

National Stepfamily Association
3rd Floor
Chapel House

18 Hatton Place
London
EC1N 8RU
Tel: Office: 0171 209 2460
Fax: 0171 209 2461
Helpline: 0990 168388

Parentline
Westbury House
57 Hart Road
Thundersly
Essex
SS7 3PD
Helpline: 01268 757077
Provides voluntary help for parents.

Relate
Herbert Gray College
Little Church Street
Rugby
Warwickshire
CV21 3AP
Tel: 01788 573 241
Fax: 01788 535 007
Relationship counselling service.

Samaritans
National Helpline: 0345 909090
Support for those who are depressed or suicidal.

Women's Aid Federation
PO Box 391
Bristol
BS99 7WS
Helpline: 0345 023468
Support and advice for women worried about violence, physical or mental.

USA

American Association of Marriage and Family Counsellors
255 Yale Avenue
Claremont
CA 917711

The Child Welfare League of America
440 1st Street, North West,
3rd Floor
Washington
DC 20001-2085
Tel: 202 638 2952
Fax: 202 638 4004

National Council on Family Relations
Central Avenue NE
550 Minneapolis
MN 55421
Tel: 612 781 9331
Fax: 612 781 9348

AUSTRALIA

Child Support Unit of Legal Aid
Western Australia
Freecall: 1800 199 363

Childcare and Accreditation Council
Central Law Courts
30 St George's Terrace
Perth
Tel: 9425 2165

Family and Children's Services
Family helpline: 9221 2000 or
Freecall: 1800 643 000

Parenting line: 9272 1466 or
Freecall: 1800 654 432

Crisis care: 9325 1111 or
Freecall: 1800 199 008

(all 24 hour information
or counselling lines)

Western Institute of Self Help (WISH)
Tel: 9228 4488 or
Freecall: 1800 195 575

Index